SUILVEN'S WORLD

A LAND AND ITS PEOPLE

Peter & Janet Sprent

NORTHWEST PRESS

Published by Northwest Press, 32 Birkhill Ave., Wormit, Newport-on-Tay, Fife, DD6 8PW, Scotland.

First published 1995

Typeset by Northwest Press.

Printed in Scotland by David Winter & Sons Ltd, Block 16, Dunsinane Avenue, Dunsinane Industrial Estate, Dundee, DD2 3QT.

ISBN 0 9524269 0 0

British Library cataloguing in publication data
A catalogue record for this book is available from the British Library.

Contents

About the authors

Peter Sprent is a retired statistician and is the author of 10 books on a variety of topics. He has broadcast on BBC Radio Scotland and local commercial radio. He is a keen hill walker and with his wife has walked extensively in *Suilven's World.*

Janet Sprent is Professor of Plant Biology at the University of Dundee and has published over 100 research papers and three books. She is a member of the UK Natural Environment Research Council and the UK Joint Nature Conservation Committee. She and her husband have made some 50 trips to *Suilven's World* during the last 20 years.

Cover photograph: Suilven from the track to Cul Mor.

Preface

This book introduces the scenic and historic wonderland between Ullapool and Kylesku that we call *Suilven's World.* We know of no single book written specifically for those who, on a first visit, find an affinity with the region and want to know more about its attractions, its history, the fascinating story of some of the oldest rock formations on earth, the plants and animals and birds of this wilderness area. There are lots of excellent books, booklets and pamphlets each dealing with parts of the region or with one specific aspect such as hill-walking, history, the geology or the flora; some deal only with named locations while others cover *Suilven's World* only as part of a greater whole, which may be the Highlands or even all Scotland. There are also many publications for specialists, be they rock climbers, geologists, or whatever.

We have tried to bridge the gap with a book that will serve as a broad introduction to visitors, or to those who have recently settled in the area. We hope you find our book a useful guide, a handy reference and a pleasing memento. To help you explore particular interests we have included a detailed further reading list. We also include in the text sources of information when we feel there are points about which you may want more detail. Our own basic information has been acquired from many sources, some clearly from published written accounts, but much of it from conversations with local residents or with experts who have studied the area.

One difficulty with historical information about this region, whether it has to do with the people, or with scientific explanations of how *Suilven's World* developed to its present form, is that of assigning dates. Written historical records are a comparatively recent innovation in the Western Highlands. Scientifically, modern techniques such as radio carbon dating or the analysis of genetic evidence have resolved many uncertainties, sometimes casting doubt upon long accepted theories. Because of such uncertainties our book is sprinkled with words like *probably* or *about*. We hope we have kept incorrect or controversial dating or claims to a minimum, but we shall be grateful to readers who detect any errors if they would point these out. Please send them to our publisher at the address given on the verso of the title page.

May we finally give a blanket thanks to all who have in conversation or by their writing provided the background information that has enabled us to tell this story in our own words. In particular we would like to thank Robert, Geraldine and Mark Irvine for the many gems of information they have passed to us over the years, and also John Riley for vetting the draft of Chapter 8, and for his many suggestions for improving it.

P.S.
J.I.S.
November, 1994

1 *Introducing Suilven's World*

A new experience

Suilven wins a deserved place on nearly everybody's list of favourite Scottish hills. It stands alone and majestic, undisputed ruler of its own little world. The geologist sees this striking massif as an island of Torridonian sandstone in a sea of ancient Lewisian gneiss. Isolation gives it an instant appeal to hillwalkers, despite the fact that it fails by some 100 feet to attain the 2500 feet needed to feature in the climbers' list of Corbetts. This leaves it far short of the Munro bagger's mandatory 3000 feet (or the less romantic metric equivalent, 914.4 m). This lack of height that denies Suilven a place in the tables compiled by Hugh T Munro in 1891, or the more modest listings by John Rooke Corbett, is more than compensated for by its solitude and grandeur.

Sometimes called 'Lochinver's mountain', Suilven, the Vikings' *Pillar Mountain,* is more than that. It dominates the view from many vantage points in Coigach and Assynt. This rocky land of mountains, hills, glens, lochs, lochans, rivers and tumbling burns is our *Suilven's World.*

We made our first trip to Wester Ross and Sutherland

a quarter century past. *Suilven's World* soon became a magnet to beckon us — usually twice, sometimes thrice — each year. Every trip has taught us more about this corner of Scotland. We want now to share our experiences, to tell of things discovered on leisurely coast or lochside strolls, on strenuous hill-walks; to pass on sometimes-disconnected bits and pieces gleaned from those who live in *Suilven's World,* either in conversation or from their writings.

The Western Highlands of Scotland may seem to be caught in a time warp. Remains of Pictish settlements lie within walking distance of modern hotels. Luxury coaches and the latest Mercedes and BMWs, humbler Peugeots, Fiats and Fords — as well as mountain bikes and Shanks's pony — bring visitors from all parts of the world to marvel at rock formations set down hundreds of millions, some thousands of millions, of years ago, and now moulded into fascinating shapes by subterranean upheavals, the scouring of ice-age glaciers and lashing wind and rain.

Tumbling stone skeletons of dwellings — roofless, doorless, windowless — once crofters' homes or abodes of earlier clansmen, stand as grim monuments to the infamous nineteenth century 'clearances'. Well engineered modern highways dissolve with stark suddenness to single-track roads with passing points, tortuous narrow winding strips of bitumen often following ill-surveyed cart- or droving-tracks of old.

But being in a time warp does not mean that time has stood still, or that there has never been change. In past millennia, today's peat bogs and heather moorlands were forests of Caledonian pine, birches, rowans, hollies, willows, junipers and alders, even some oaks. Had there been roads 4000 years ago, sheep lazing or grazing in your path would not have been a problem. You might instead have found your right-of-way challenged by wolves or blocked by an elegant reindeer, perhaps even a brown bear or a lynx.

The Highlands have indeed changed with time; it is only the pace and tempo of that change that differs from that in other parts of Britain. That there have been, sometimes dramatic, transformations is sometimes forgotten by ardent conservationists intent upon preserving the status quo. Some changes have been man-made, but many have been responses to whims of nature. Humans now have a greater potential for changing the environment — for better or worse — than ever before. We must use that potential wisely in sensitive environments. That is why bodies like the recently formed Scottish Natural Heritage — and its predecessor, the Nature Conservancy — have, and are, playing such an active, and one hopes increasingly influential role, in studying and making recommendations about highly interactive natural systems. These bodies take, we are happy to say, a more balanced view of the problems than some well-meaning individuals and pressure groups with gazes understandably, but often unfortunately, riveted on only one aspect of problems that have many interacting facets.

A fickle climate

As full of surprises as the land itself is Highland weather. In a 1970s brochure, now-retired Achiltibuie hotelier Robert Irvine wrote:

> *We have the Gulf Stream at the foot of the crofts, but the weather can be anything from Arctic to Aegean inside a week.*

He might have said *sometimes inside a day*, though that does not happen very often. A capricious climate explains, in part at least, why the hills look that little different each day and why walking across a peaty moor, on one day an easy stroll, may on the next be a frustrating slog, feet sinking three, even six or more, inches into mud at each step. Sadly, too, sudden unexpected changes in weather here — as in other parts of the Highlands — have contributed to walking accidents on even seemingly docile hills. But never let the weather get you down, for a quirky climate is a major creative element for an ever-changing kaleidoscope that lends an ethereal romanticism to this land of lochs and hills.

How one spends the day in *Suilven's World* — be it walking, fishing, interspersing driving with an occasional stroll by shore, lochside, bank of burn or river, putting photographic skills to the test, studying some of the world's oldest rock formations, bird-watching or botanizing — may influence the way evenings are spent. Many keep a close communion with nature by pitching a tent or retreating to their own, or a hired, caravan. Others seek bed and breakfast, perhaps dinner, too, in a croft — hoping to learn about local attractions and hear some of the history and legends of *Suilven's World* first-hand from natural story-tellers with a lifetime's experience, many of them skilled raconteurs happy to pass on stories of their youth and to retell legends handed down from generation to generation. There is a wealth of folklore, some linked to historical events, others like the legend of the Yellow Boy (from whence Achiltibuie is supposed by some to take its name) shrouded in mystery as obscure as mountain mist. Some visitors to the Highlands opt for a self-catering chalet or holiday cottage; others seek an hotel, often one where kindred spirits — be they hillwalkers, fishermen, geologists, historians, or botanists — are known to congregate. Such hostelries range from convivial, modest yet comfortable, inns, to hotels with an international reputation for food and wines; there are at least two of the latter in, or near, our *Suilven's World*.

We write about the activities one may enjoy, describe the region's attractions, its history, its flora, fauna and geology; tell the story of its people. We want to whet your appetite for a closer exploration of *Suilven's World*. For visitors we hope that in later years our book will also rekindle pleasant memories of what is often an all-too-short stay in this corner of the Highlands and that it will enable you to share your experiences with friends who do not know this historic land. If you are one of the many who have settled in these parts in recent years, we hope we have something new to tell you about your adopted home. Not everything that interests us will appeal to you — it would be a dull world if we all had the same tastes — but we have tried to make this a friendly, not too formal, handy reference. The reading list on p.145 includes a few more formal guides, and doubtless you will come across others, ranging from pamphlets to fully-fledged books on topics of interest. Some of the books we have listed are, unfortunately, now out of print (most publishers these days are run by accountants, not booklovers), but we have included them because they are useful books, and you may know a friend who has a copy or stumble upon one in a library or in a second-hand bookstore.

Finding Suilven

Have you heard the heresy that 'there's nothing north of Ullapool'? If so, it will quickly be dispelled, no matter whether you take the road north from that 200-year-old fishing town on Loch Broom, or come to our Suilven's World by Ledmore from the east or Kylesku from the north. From Ullapool, when you top the hill just a mile beyond that town, the wall-like mass of Ben Mor Coigach lies ahead, giving from this aspect little hint that part of its ridge is almost a knife-edge. A little further on, near the camp, caravan and boating site at Ardmair Point, looking beyond the bird sanctuary of Isle Martin, you see the impressive plunge of the Coigach range to the shore of Loch Broom. Other towering mountains soon appear — Cul Beag and beyond it the even solider mass of Cul Mor. Next you see the rocky pinnacles

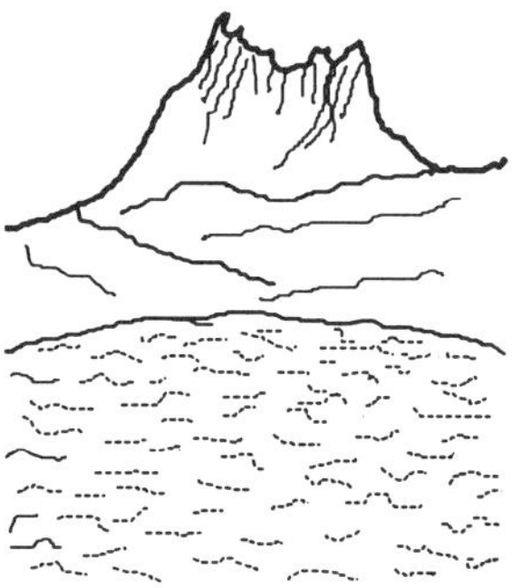

of Scotland's famed mountain in miniature, Stac Pollaidh, conventionally anglicised to Stac Polly.

Be patient. Your first glimpse of Suilven, nature's ruler of this little world, comes later, no matter whether you follow the main inland road through Elphin, Ledmore and Inchnadamph to Lochinver or Kylesku; or if, ten miles north of Ullapool you opt at the one-house-plus-AA-telephone settlement of Drumrunie, for the single track road to Achiltibuie that leads also to the coast route to Lochinver by the aptly named 'wee mad road'.

The inland route gives a first glimpse of Suilven as you enter Elphin soon after passing the Knockan Cliffs, while the Achiltibuie road gives inspiring vistas of lochs and a close-up of Stac Pollaidh as you skirt Loch Lurgainn, but keeps you waiting that little bit longer for Suilven. But your reward comes if you ignore the turning for Lochinver some nine miles after leaving the main road, and head instead towards Achiltibuie. Look back to your right after crossing a cattle grid and then a bridge over the Garvie River that tumbles from Loch Osgaig the few hundred yards north to Enard Bay and you will see Suilven in glorious full-frontal nudity. Stop one-third to one-half of a mile further on and again look back to admire a magnificent panorama; Quinag to the north, with its three main and several subsidiary peaks, then clockwise east stands Suilven, with close behind and almost hidden, a glimpse of Canisp. Further east then south Cul Mor towers behind Stac Pollaidh and Cul Beag rises to the right; across Loch Osgaig in the foreground are the twin

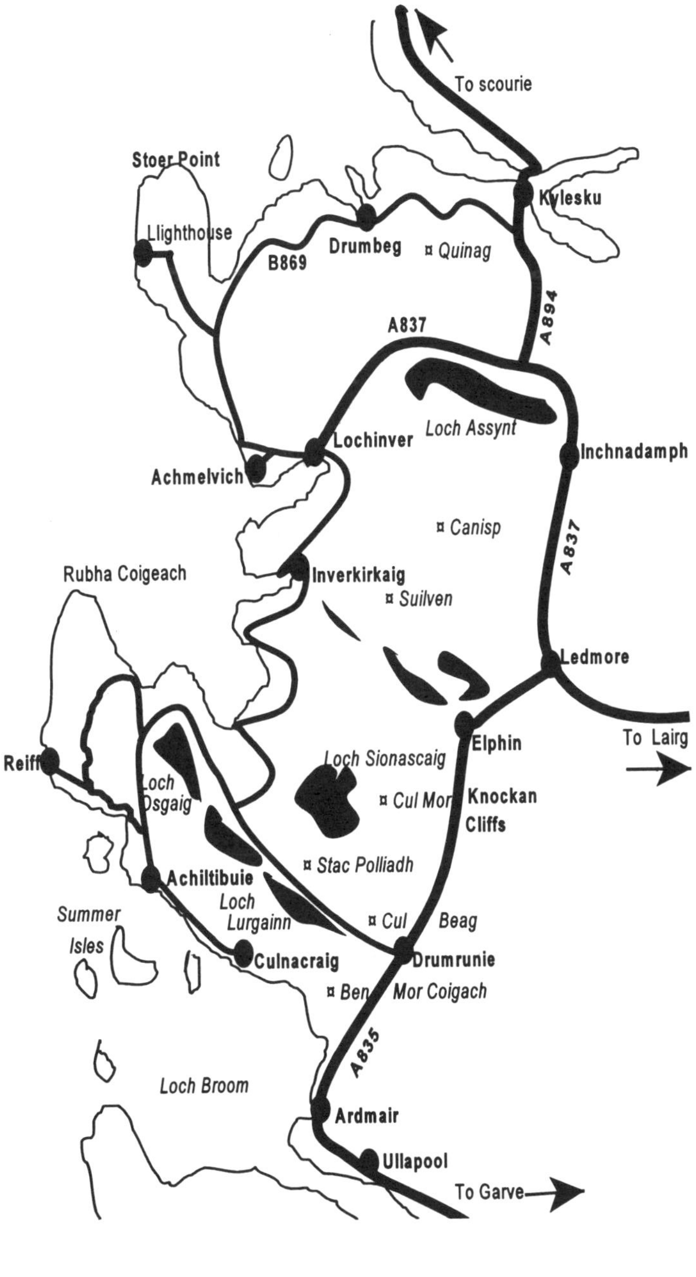
To scourie
Stoer Point
Kylesku
Llighthouse
Drumbeg
Quinag
B869
A894
A837
Loch Assynt
Lochinver
Inchnadamph
Achmelvich
Canisp
A837
Rubha Coigeach
Inverkirkaig
Suilven
Ledmore
To Lairg
Elphin
Reiff
Loch Osgaig
Loch Sionascaig
Cul Mor
Knockan Cliffs
Stac Polliadh
Achiltibuie
Summer Isles
Loch Lurgainn
Cul Beag
Culnacraig
Drumrunie
Ben Mor Coigach
A835
Loch Broom
Ardmair
Ullapool
To Garve

peaks of Beinn an Eoin and behind these lie the Coigach hills, the most striking of which, from this aspect — and indeed from many points on the Achiltibuie road — is Sgurr an Fhidhleir, referred to more often as 'The Fiddler', its pointed summit atop a sheer cliff.

If you come this far on the coast route you may well go on to Achiltibuie. In the next chapter, we say more about this and the 'wee mad road' to Lochinver and the coast road through Drumbeg that rejoins the main road north a few miles short of Kylesku.

The main road north through Elphin and Ledmore junction — where you enter *Suilven's World* if you come from Bonar Bridge or Lairg — and on to Inchnadamph has scenically a little less to offer than the coastal route, but interpret our 'little less' to mean 'still plenty'. You see the same mountains, pass the beautiful and historic Loch Assynt from where a road runs west to Lochinver (the fast road to this thriving fishing port) while the other branch continues north to Kylesku, Scourie and beyond. Those who enter *Suilven's World* from the north do so by the sweeping arc of the Kylesku bridge, opened only in 1984, and so well blended to the landscape that it won its designers a richly-deserved and prestigious architectural award.

It is time now to explore Coigach and Assynt in more detail. The ideal map for all but the southern strip of *Suilven's World* is the 1:50 000 Ordnance Survey (OS) Landranger map, sheet 15: *Loch Assynt & surrounding area.* A few places we mention are not on sheet 15; Ullapool, for example is on sheet 19. To help you find places on these maps we give in later chapters grid references for places we mention. A typical reference look like this — NC 094225 — and we described how they are formed and used with the Landranger maps in Appendix A on p.137. We hope you find them useful.

2 Things to do

A bit about the place

If you have already planned the basics of your visit to *Suilven's World,* or if that is where you live, there may be little in this chapter that you do not already know. But if you come afresh to the area, some of this routine information may prove helpful. That is why we have designed this chapter as a conventional thumb-nail sketch about things that most people want to know about a locality. We leave special interests — walking, angling, botanizing, bird-watching, rock studies, historical and archaeological expeditions — to later chapters, matched more directly to specific interests. Please tune your reading of the chapter to match your needs for background information.

Most people come to the Western Highlands by car, coach, motorcycle, pedal their way on a mountain bike, walk or hitch-hike. A few have been known to drop from the skies in their private helicopter. There are buses and scheduled coach services linking Ullapool with Inverness, but few visitors rely on public transport as their sole means of locomotion, although there are some scheduled, mostly post- or school-bus, services between centres within the Coigach and Assynt districts. Understandably, in the light of their prime functions, these often run at times not ideally suited to sightseeing, though residents and visitors sometimes find them handy.

Because the Highland tourist industry is largely seasonal — mainly from about Easter to October, commercial enterprises like hotels, guest houses, crofts that offer bed and breakfast (B&B) or dinner, bed and breakfast (DB&B), camping and caravan sites, as well as craft and souvenir shops and other local facilities may alter the services they provide or change hands — even disappear — between seasons. It is to cope with such changes that national guides for hotels, restaurants, budget-eating, B&B, camping and caravanning, are published annually. Use current editions of a guide that matches your needs. To avoid giving what may quickly become out-dated advice, we omit details about specific places or enterprises apart from a few — many to us 'old friends'— that are well established and seem likely to remain part of the scene. Sometimes we may get this wrong; but we hope not often.

Before turning to things to do, some remarks about accommodation may help your planning. There is accomodation to suit all tastes at prices from top hotel rates to a nominal fee for the right to pitch your tent, but in the peak tourist season it is no fun to find at 7 p.m. that you have nowhere to sleep. Accommodation and other information is available at the Tourist Offices in Ullapool (NH 128939) or Lochinver (NC 094225). If the grid reference system, Appendix A, is new to you, these examples may help you check whether you have come to grips with it.

If you seek an hotel, Ullapool, the southern entry-point to *Suilven's World*, has a range, some long established, some newer, catering between them for nearly all tastes. Two have unusual features; the first is not, strictly speaking, in Ullapool, indeed it is not even accessible by road; one must cross Loch Broom by the hotel's own boat to reach Fred Brown and Gunn Eriksen's *Altnaharrie Inn* (NH 115930). This eight-bedroom hotel, with prices to match its reputation, has won deserved and lavish praise for foods and wines in leading hotel and restaurant guides.

An opera house or concert hall in Ullapool, Elphin or Lochinver would be as out of place as a croft in London's Regent Street, but Ullapool's pleasantly off-beat and enterprising *Ceilidh Place* features entertainment by local and visiting performers of a kind inspired by, or perhaps that provided the inspiration for, that centre's name. Some of these artists and artistes also perform in remoter village halls from time to time. Not only is the *Ceilidh Place* (NH 126940) an entertainment centre, but this pleasantly informal complex is the town's attempt to be all things to nearly all men and women; it includes an hotel and restaurant together with a 'club house' providing simpler accommodation; there is a coffee-shop, too, that serves meals and snacks from breakfast to evening, and to round it all off, also a bookshop.

For number of hotels, Lochinver, at the heart of *Suilven's World,* comes second only to Ullapool. Here, the modern *Inver Lodge Hotel* (NC 095224) offers high standard accommodation — and a fine view of Suilven (NC 154184).

Kylesku (NC 230337), Inchnadamph (NC 251216) and Achitibuie (NC 025085) all boast popular but individualistic hotels. Kylesku Hotel is adjacent to the old ferry slipway, a site that offers some of the finest fjord-like scenery in Scotland, with views up the twin Lochs Glencoul and Glendhu and it is popular with those who, after a day of outdoor activity, look forward to good food in a convivial atmosphere. Inchnadamph hotel, close to historic Loch Assynt, has long been a favourite with fishermen, geologists and hill-walkers.

Achiltibuie's *Summer Isles Hotel* (NC 026081) is a favourite of ours. A small hotel, it is ideal for those who love good food and wine and a comfortable bed after a day's sight-seeing, a walk on coast or hills, or a challenging day's fishing on river or loch. We found this hotel in

1974, and have been regular visitors for 20 years. Like the *Altnaharrie Inn*, it has an international reputation for food, and a fine wine list. Here in 1994 we enjoyed a 1979 Grand Cru Chateau Yon-Figeac at the bargain price, for a restaurant, of £25 a bottle. Sorry, wine lovers, we put our minds to ensuring that stocks are now exhausted, but look out for comparable joys on the extensive list.

When we first knew it, the *Summer Isles* was run by Robert Irvine and his partner Roberta. Robert's daughter, Lucy, later to win fame as authoress of the best-selling *Castaway* was also part of the team in those early days. In the 1980s Robert left to concentrate on horticultural experiments across the road in the *Hydroponicum* (NC 026080) and the hotel is now in the capable hands of Robert's son Mark and his wife, Geraldine.

Not everbody wants to stay in hotels. Throughout *Suilven's World,* many visitors favour B&B or DB&B establishments. These abound, ranging from guest houses to private homes, farmhouses and, sometimes isolated, crofts. Some have Scottish Tourist Board approval, and prices are often well below those charged at hotels and often represent excellent value for money. An added attraction of B&B in homes and crofts may be the opportunity for an evening chat about the area with local residents as 'part of the family'. Although some of these places belong to recent incomers to the area, many of these owners, like us, have become keen students of local history and folklore.

Holiday cottages and self-catering chalets are scattered throughout Coigach and Assynt, especially in coastal areas; the size, facilities and furnishings provided are usually reflected in the rentals.

Camping and caravanning is popular in *Suilven's World,* with well-known sites at Ardmair Point (NH 109985) near Ullapool, at Achmelvich (NC 054248) and at Clachtoll (NC 041273), both the latter a few miles north of Lochinver (NC 095225); these, and other sites, are usually busy in the peak tourist months of July and August. At some sites 'fixed' caravans are available for hire. Camping and overnight parking of caravans is not allowed in the Inverpolly Nature Reserve (NC 140120).

If you bring your own caravan, especially if it is a trailer, remember that a few single track roads in the Western Highlands are unsuitable for these. Even on those not so classified, driving skill is needed to reverse a trailer caravan to a passing point when faced by on-coming traffic. A few thoughtless caravan owners assume other drivers will appreciate their problem and do any necessary backing. The flaw in that logic is brutally exposed when two caravan owners who have both made this assumption meet head on.

There are Youth Hostels at Acheninver (NC 043057), some two miles beyond Achiltibuie and south of the dead-end road to Culnacraig, and also at Achmelvich (NC 059248).

At the height of the season demand for accommodation is heavy, so advanced booking is advisable. In spring and autumn (except at Easter) bookings are lighter, and both are good times to visit the area. May is usually particularly pleasant and the weather often more settled than in the summer, but we offer no guarantees!

For your enjoyment

What about features worth visiting and exploring in *Suilven's World*? We assume you have your own transport, sophisticated or basic, and are prepared in a few cases also to do some not-too-strenuous, walking. Serious walking and hill climbing are the subjects of Chapter 3.

We cover special activities in later chapters, but this leaves lots of things to do and places to visit — as well as simply relaxing and enjoying the scenery. We look at some possibilities on a district-by-district basis. As we did for accommodation, we only name specific enterprises we believe to be well established, but changes are still possible so check locally if you plan a special trip to such a facility. A husband-and-wife artist and weaver combination we thought firmly settled sold their business to take up new activities while we were writing this book.

Ullapool (NH 128939)

Anne Barnes, in an informative booklet on the town (see our Further Reading list, p.145), describes the Ullapool of 200 years ago as *a brand new Milton Keynes of the 1780s*. Before that it was only a farm. It grew as a fishing port; but it is debatable today whether it is basically still that, or is now primarily a tourist centre. The hub of activity is the area near the pier, although the steamer that at the beginning of this century carried steerage-class passengers on the three-day trip to Glasgow for a mere three shillings no longer plies. The only major ferry service from the modern Ullapool is that by the now-ageing *Suilven* — named, of course, after our mountain — on a twice-daily run to Stornaway on the isle of Lewis.

Ullapool is not a spectacular town, yet one of charm. Neat cottages, many whitewashed and of varying age, line a rect-angular grid of streets. Founded in 1788 on the initiative of the British Fisheries Society to encourage fishing for the herring then abundant in Loch Broom, the settlement was well planned and has developed with gradually changing emphases since that date. It has known bleak times. In 1847, the herring having by then apparently deserted Loch Broom, the Fisheries Society sold Ullapool for £5000, then a lot of money, but well below the sum it had invested in it. A hundred years later the Garve to Ullapool road was still mostly single track, and earlier this century it had only a gravel surface. Although road improvements spelt doom for the coastal steamers to Glasgow, easier access encouraged a tourist industry that alleviated growing fears about the future of commercial fishing. As herring stocks in Loch Broom, and later beyond, were depleted, fishermen had to search ever further afield and turn to other species to supplement dwindling supplies. Something of a miniboom has taken place in the last two decades with the coming of East European factory ships — the klondikers — hungry for supplies of mackerel for processing. At certain times of year fleets of these klondikers — many rusted relics of better days — anchor in the loch not only close to the pier, but as far out as abeam the Summer Isles. Local fishermen have found a ready sale for their catches, and the ships' crews on shore leave have been eager purchasers of Western consumer goods and enthusiastic patrons of local cafés and restaurants.

Some of Ullapool's buildings date back to the heyday of fishing, although now put to different uses. The tourist office and MacBrayne's Ferry office are in the old *Red Herring Shed,* where once the herring were salted and hung over oak fires for several weeks until they became red (no dyes used in those days!).

Like all places that attract tourists, Ullapool has many souvenir shops supplying local or typically Scottish goods (and sadly at a few, sometimes imported items of questionable relevance as souvenirs). The Highland Stoneware company designs, manufactures and sells attractive pottery both here and at its main factory in Lochinver. It makes fish dishes of appropriate shapes and in sizes suitable both as wall decorations or for serving trout and small or large whole salmon. These are supplemented by a variety of bowls, vases, cheese dishes, etc. to suit most tastes and credit card limits. Several hotels and restaurants serve local produce, especially seafoods. Indeed, lovers of shellfish are well catered for both in Ullapool and Lochinver.

The museum is in the old Ullapool Church, built in 1829. It lies between the post office and *The Ceilidh Place* in West Argyle Street and contains not only a collection of memorabilia of the town's historical development but also has an *Emigration Corner* displaying many documents relevant to, and correspondence with or about, those who left the district for Canada, Australia and New Zealand — migrations often connected with the infamous 'clearances' (Chapter 4).

Cruises to the Summer Isles and fishing trips depart from the pier throughout the season.

The Highlands have always attracted artists; some challenged by an urge to record the dramatic changes of mood induced by a fickle climate. Many have worked to record that blend of scenic beauty, oft hostile nature and economic hardship that has shaped Highland life-style. Others have had an eye only for the grandeur and majesty of rugged mountains, the sometimes peaceful but often wind-swept lochs, and tumbing burns. Several artists with sharply contrasting styles, some who have exhibited nationally or internationally, have studios in *Suilven's World* where their works are for sale. These and others talented with pencil or brush also exhibit from time to time at the *Ceilidh Place* in Ullapool and in other hotels, restaurants, cafés and craft shops throughout the region. Talented weavers, too, produce a range of knitwear as well as attractive tapestries and wall or floor mats depicting highland scenes. These are sold in craft shops in Ullapool and the rest of the area, sometimes even from the 'homes' where they are created during long northern winter evenings.

Artist James Hawkins moved to a small croft at Rhue, north of Ullapool, in 1978 and there set up in a small outbuilding, the Rhue Studio (NH 101969), which he has gradually improved to provide good viewing facilities for his work. The modest sign where the short spur to Rhue branches from the main road (A835) two miles north from Ullapool gives only a slight hint that this is the base for an artist who exhibits regularly at leading galleries in Edinburgh, Glasgow and London and as far afield as Berlin. Let him speak for himself:

> *The themes of my work have been developed through a rigorous dialogue between observation of natural details and endless experiments with painted, collaged and printed surfaces . . ..*
> *Images of landscapes hover in a web of marks which is tantalisingly short of complete, ensuring that no single interpretation can dominate; but rather a continual re-assessment occurs*

The abstract nature of much of Hawkins' works does not appeal to everyone. With a twinkle in his eye he explains that a few orthodox sketches and some of his more straightforward water colours are done to convince doubters that he really possesses the basic skills needed to express visual reality on board or canvas.

James Hawkins' major paintings are certainly *'tantalisingly short of complete'*. We own several; one, acquired more than a decade ago, leaves us still undecided whether a swirl of greyish-white is cloud or a snow-clad mountain glimpsed through mist; and whether the scene depicts the depths of winter or just a passing summer storm.

Coigach

Coigach literally means 'place of the fifths', said by some to refer to one-fifth of a *davach*, or *davoch*, an old Scottish land measure of some 416 acres. This hardly seems relevant to the present district which covers roughly that part of Wester Ross to the west of the main road north from Ardmair (NH 111984) through Strath Kanaird (NC 151020) to Drumrunie and on to the Sutherland border at NC 193096.

On our early trips we sped north to Lochinver or to the old Kylesku ferry, now replaced by that fine curving bridge (NC 227338), en route to points north. In 1974, for the first time, we turned left just ten miles out of Ullapool at Drumrunie (NC 166053) on the single track Achiltibuie trail. Here Stac Pollaidh (NC 108106) becomes ever more impressive as the contorted road winds down to Loch Lurgainn (NC 110090). On a fine day, a crowded car-park (NC 108095) at the base of what looks a stiff climb bears testimony to the popularity of this isolated rocky tor. For the fit, the ascent to the ridge takes less than an hour, but be sure you are suitably clad before attempting the walk, which we describe more fully in the next chapter. The climb is not without challenge, but the only twinge of regret is likely to be triggered by all too obvious evidence of the erosive potential of walking boots.

At a junction (NC 063112) beyond the Stac a single-track road, sensibly designated '*unsuitable for coaches and caravans*', climbs sharp-right. Sign-posted *Lochinver,* this is the famous 'wee mad road', a 'must' for all whose stay extends to more than just a day.

If you head for Achiltibuie, driving now becomes that little less exacting as the road untangles itself to near-straight on its northern traverse of Loch Osgaig (NC 045120). In the season, if weather favours the fisherman, Osgaig is a place to admire, or, depending on your philosophy perhaps to be puzzled by, the near-infinite patience of anglers as they try their skills from bank or boat on this, one of the Coigach district's more popular fishing lochs. Near Osgaig's western extremity, after crossing a cattle grid, a bridge (NC 040130) spans the River Garvie — an impatient torrent that cascades the waters of the Loch the few hundred yards north to Enard Bay.

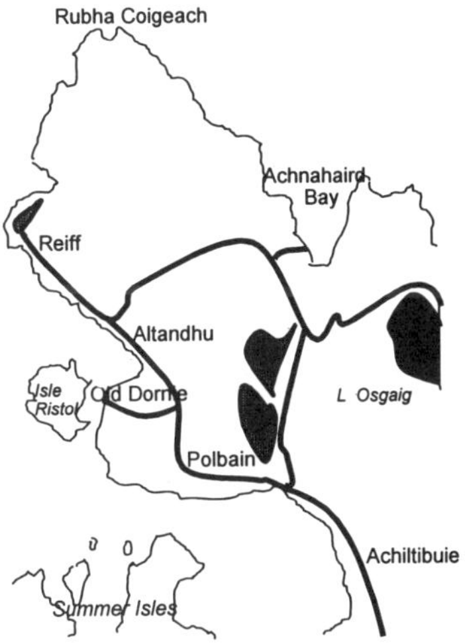

A mile or so past the Garvie, the road makes an easy winding descent; to the right the pure sands of Achnahaird beach (NC 019138) (Plate II) catch the eye; if the wind is from the prevailing west or north-west, its attraction enhanced by a pounding surf. At the foot of the brae one has a choice of routes; on our first trip, time was short so we bore left for the ten-minute drive direct to Achiltibuie. We often prefer now to fork right for a scenic detour via the Rubha Coigeach peninsula; savouring, several miles on, a spectacular view of the Summer Isles as the road winds down towards Altandhu (NB 980130). If time permits — and time is plentiful in the Western Highlands — and we are mooded to dally, at the Altandhu junction we turn right again for Rieff (NB 966144), a road-end settlement some two miles on. To the north, on the Scottish mainland, there is no other habitation so far west. In fair weather we often park near the road-end and pass a leisurely half hour or more strolling across the turf to the rocky western shore beyond the tiny — but not very impressive — Loch of Rieff. In all but the driest weather we don good stout shoes or boots even for this easy walk, and if there is a chill wind off the sea we take an anorak or maybe a tougher defence against bracing Atlantic, sometimes Arctic, breezes.

On return one must back-track to Altandhu, from where a road runs direct to Achiltibuie. This road passes the *Summer Isles Smokehouse*, (NB 988124) whose local products have won an international market. Visitors are welcome to inspect, and buy, during working hours. Beyond the Smokehouse, if one has an urge for a further short detour, a side road to the right leads to Old Dornie Harbour (NB 983112), a convenient shelter for local fishing boats and lying opposite Isle Ristol, the Summer Isle closest to the mainland. A short climb over the hill at Polbain (NB 994102), brings one to sprawling Achiltibuie with its crofts, cottages and increasing numbers of holiday and retirement homes. A mile or so after entering the village, one reaches the already-mentioned *Summer Isles Hotel*, transformed by ex-London-film-producer Robert Irvine and his partner Roberta about 1970 from a somewhat modest base. Nearly opposite is the *Hydroponicum,* monument to Robert's flirtation with science. His revolutionary horticultural experiments — growing plants in nutrient solutions rather than soil and making best use of long hours of sunshine filtered through modern translucent screening — won world attention, but it has had its ups and downs, and the building is not in line for any Charlie boy (or other) architectural awards. Conducted tours of the hydroponicum have been available for some years, and visitors have been amazed that, with the methods pioneered by Robert Irvine, it is possible not only to produce ripe strawberries in May, even sometimes in April, but also to grow bananas at a latitude of 58°N.

Achiltibuie is an excellent centre for both fishermen and walkers. As well as angling on loch or river (Chapter 9), sea fishing cruises are available by arrangement from Achiltibuie or Ullapool.

In the season there are regular cruises from the Badentarbat pier (NC 008096) at Achiltibuie, as well as from Ullapool, to the Summer Isles. Many of these allow time ashore on Tanera Beag (NB 965075) or Tanera Mor (NB 990073), the latter the only Isle still with permanent residents, and the site of a fish farm, the cages in the bay being clearly visible from Achiltibuie when the light is right. Tanera Mor was for some years before and during the second world war the home of the noted Scottish naturalist and author F Fraser Darling. At the beginning of the century the island had a larger population and its own thriving school. In the 1970s its then owner tried to stimulate tourism by issuing Summer Isles postage stamps, valid only for internal mail on the islands! Several of the islands are used for grazing and most attract itinerant bird-watchers and naturalists, both profess-ional and amateur. Fraser Darling and others have found Priest Island (NB 925022), which is a designated site of special scientific interest, a fascinating haunt for studying natural history. Seals bask on the rocks on many of the islands; these and numerous sea-birds, are highlights of any cruise, so do not forget your binoculars. In her booklet *The Summer Isles*, Anne Barnes lists about 40 birds that may be seen on the Isles.

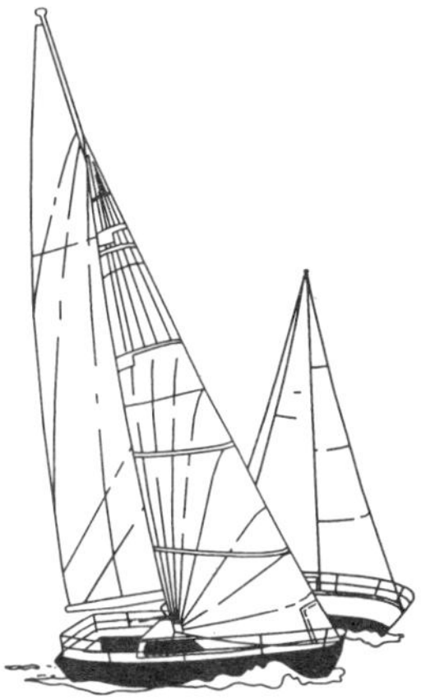

Even inshore waters are often choppy on a breezy day, so if your sea legs are a little jelly-like, choose a calm day for a cruise. Take warm clothing too, no matter how good the weather when you set out, for a breeze may spring up with little notice, or rain may sweep in from the Atlantic with only minutes of warning.

Why are they called the Summer Isles? We have heard three explanations, but can vouch for none. The commonest is that the name reflects a long-established use for summer grazing of sheep and cattle. However, it has also been suggested that an even earlier use was for winter grazing of Highland cattle, and that with this in mind someone with an impish sense of humour may have bestowed the name. A more likely explanation is that the name is, like some others along this coast, and more particularly in the Northern and Western Isles, of Viking origin, for it is known that the Norsemen once visited, indeed settled on the Summer Isles. Anne Barnes, this time in her booklet *Achiltibuie* (Eagle-eye Press, 1989) suggests the name could be a corruption of the Norse *Simmer Skit* meaning boundary isles, the isles being regarded as a boundary between the Hebrides and the mainland. She claims there is evidence that they were called the Simmer Isles in the early 18th century, though no group name is given to the Isles in a map in Blaeu's 17th century *Atlas Novus*.

Inverkirkaig and Lochinver

From Achiltibuie the way out, like the way in, is past Loch Osgaig towards Ullapool, at least as far as the junction (NC 063112) with that 'wee mad road' to Lochinver. This 'outward' drive is more spectacular than the inward one, giving that panoramic view of mountains from Quinag (NC 209292) to the Coigach hills that we described on p.14. Now one does not have to turn round to admire it.

Despite its unsuitability for coaches and caravans, for the ordinary car driver the 'mad' road demands only commonsense care and ability to reverse to a passing point on a narrow winding tarmac strip. The most difficult section is a quarter-mile stretch (NC 075176) around the small anchorage at the north-eastern extremity of Enard Bay. Here contortions of the road just feet above the shoreline at the base of a steepish hillside limit forward visibility sometimes to a few yards, so be ready to pull up short when faced by on-coming traffic. Take care if you have to back to a passing point, for sharp rocks millions of years old have no respect for today's thin car body shells. Scenery on this road is for passenger enjoyment, but alas, not for the driver, as the turns and undulations that bring the kaleidoscope of seascapes, mountain views and glimpses of lochs demand a driver's full attention. At the right time of day — usually early morning or towards evening — on this road we have spotted deer and a variety of birds, including buzzards. It is buzzards, not golden eagles, that sit atop electricity or telephone poles.

In the glen northeast of the Inverpolly salmon hatchery (NC 074134) in April or early May, carpets of wild primroses add a splash of delicate yellow to grassy wooded slopes.

Inverkirkaig (NC 078198) settlement is on the sea loch, but by a bridge over the Kirkaig some half-mile upstream before the settlement is reached, there is a landscaped car-park (NC 086193) usually known as the Inverkirkaig car-park, unobtrusive but woefully inadequate on a fine summer's day.

Inverkirkaig's one shop — a combined bookshop, woven goods and coffee shop — is near this car-park. A steep path leads the 100 yards or so to Achins, and you may drive up to the entrance, but space is limited, so you will win no friends if you leave your car here after you have finished shopping or taking refreshment. Achins stocks more than the usual collection of tourist books, national and local, found in conventional souvenir shops. Books range from those on local history and the attractions of the area, through general Scottish fiction and non-fiction to the classics and crime and other popular works for both adults and children, as well as a supply of reference books. If you have no appropriate maps of the area, make good your deficiency here. Local paintings and sketches are displayed and there is a range of knitwear, too. Home-baked cakes and scones and light snacks at lunch-time in the coffee shop are welcome in an area once bereft of such offerings.

Inverkirkaig car-park is the start for the popular walk to Kirkaig Falls (NC 111179), (Plate I) that we say more about in the next chapter. The walk explains, in part, the often crowded car-park, but its patrons also include, in season, those fishing the Kirkaig river and it is one possible starting point for a day-long climb of Suilven. The river marks the border between the old counties of Wester Ross and Sutherland, the administrator's imaginary bisecting line for *Suilven's World.*

Literally, Inverkirkaig means the site of the church by the river mouth, and there was once a monastery here, an 11th century settlement where the monks were allowed to marry, but their wives lived separately at Badnaban (NC 080209) — the grove of the women — about one mile north.

It is only a few miles from Inverkirkaig to the attractive fishing and tourist centre of Lochinver (NC 094225). Just before entering that village by the 'wee mad road' one passes the local school, at the edge of tiny Loch Culag (NC 096217). With, in the middle distance Suilven peeping over the nearer hills, this must be one of the most beautifully sited schools on earth. Is any work done here? The temptation to look out the window must be almost irresistible.

Beyond the school, the Culag River races headlong over boulders to the sea loch from which Lochinver settlement takes its name. At the northern end of the village the river Inver itself tumbles, almost as impatiently, into the loch.

Lochinver has changed a lot in the 25 years we have known it. An injection of European Community money for new fish-landing and processing facilities has boosted the economy, but to claim it has added little of aesthetic appeal is putting it charitably, although the excavations it involved are slowly mellowing into the surroundings. Tourist facilities — accommodation, shopping and banking — have all expanded. Shops range from a small super-market to those specializing in food, newspapers, ironmongery and ship's chandlery. There is currently a bistro-type restaurant with take-away facilities. The Highland Stoneware pottery (NC 093230) is the town's main industry after fishing and tourism, and there is a small general industrial estate on the main route to Ullapool or the north.

The coast road north

The main road to and from Lochinver, the A837, provides quick entry or exit, but if time is not too pressing, the attractive route north is the coast road to Stoer (NC 039286), Drumbeg (NC 125325) and Kylesku (NC 230337). Driverwise, particularly after the 'wee mad road' this is relatively easy, though largely single-track, as far as Drumbeg. Onward from there it acquires some of the characteristics of its southern counterpart.

A few miles north of Lochinver a side road leads to the coast at Achmelvich (NC 057246), a popular camping spot with a fine beach, but despite the Gulf Stream only the hardy (or foolhardy) are tempted to swim here. Beyond the small settlements of Clachtoll (NC 041273) and Stoer, another branch road leads to Stoer lighthouse (NC 004330), perched on cliffs less than two miles south of the Point of Stoer (NC 021356). The lighthouse, built by the Stevenson brothers in 1870, is now automated. The cliffs between the lighthouse and the point are at their most impressive when pounded by breakers in a westerly gale. The more energetic may walk north from the lighthouse to the point over, often boggy, ground to see one of Scotland's many coastal 'stacs' — *The Old Man of Stoer* (NC 016353) — featured in the 1994 BBC television series *The Edge* about famous Scottish climbs and climbers. Take care on this walk, because the sheer cliffs drop 100 feet or more in many places, and only experienced and well equipped rock climbers should try to descend them. The 'Old Man' itself is strictly for the experts.

On the coastal route between Lochinver and Drumbeg, there are numerous lochans, often in pans scored out by ice age glaciers, and in late summer and early autumn many of these are a mass of flowering water-lilies. There is a clearly signposted viewpoint (NC 120330) as you enter Drumbeg. Stop here a few moments to admire the fine sea and coastal view northward. After Drumbeg the twisting road generates alternating views of the western flank of Quinag and the island-studded Eddrachillis Bay. Beyond the sheltered anchorage of Loch Nedd, after hairpin descents and ascents as it crosses Gleann Ardbhair (NC 184331), the route skirts the northern flank of Quinag to join the main road to the far-north, the A894, at NC 232314, several miles south of Kylesku. It is worth turning left and heading north to cross the Kylesku bridge (NC 227338). Pause in the car-park beyond the bridge to enjoy the fjord-like views up the twin lochs Glendhu and Glencoul. A return by the outward route will not disappoint, especially if one can change drivers so that someone else has to concentrate on this all-important matter.

In summer, boat trips from the old ferry landing stage at Kylesku (NC 230338) up Loch Glencoul, give not only a close view of the Glencoul thrust (Plate V), a prominent and famous geological feature we say more about in Chapter 5, but also a good, if slightly distant, view of Eas a' Chual Aluinn (NC 280277), Britain's highest waterfall with a drop in two steps of over 600 feet, some three times the height of the Niagara Falls, though the volume comparison is less flattering. In his book, *The Waterfalls of Scotland*, Louis Scott records the folk tale of a maiden who hid in the nearby cliffs from a suitor she did not love and when he pursued her, threw herself from the cliff and her tresses spread out to form the waterfall, giving rise to a locally used name, *The Maiden's Tresses*, for the falls.

Inchnadamph and Loch Assynt

The main road from Kylesku south to Ullapool joins the fast road from Lochinver at Skiag Bridge (NC 235243) by Loch Assynt.

At Skiag Bridge it takes the number, A837, of the Ledmore to Lochinver road. Inchnadamph (NC 250217) is a centre for those interested in geology, archaeology or history. We give details in the relevant chapters, but the historical focus is the crumbling ruins of Ardvreck castle (NC 240237) on a low spit that juts into Loch Assynt some half mile southeast of Skiag Bridge. Nearby are the remains of Calda House (NC 244234), a scene of clan feuding in the 18th century. Heed the warnings to keep clear of both because of the fragile condition of the remaining walls. The rock at Inchnadamph is limestone, and this has led to the formation of underground and hillside caves. The entrances to some are accessible by short walks from Inchnadamph, but only experienced potholers of cave explorers should go underground. In a group of caves in a limestone cliff (NC 268170), close to the Allt nan Uamh, known as the *Bone Caves*, archaeologists some 70 years ago discovered human bones and those of reindeer and animals now long extinct in these parts, including bears and lynx. Even earlier, two geologists famous for their explorations in this area, Benjamin Peach and John Horne, had found in these caves evidence of the use of fire by primitive settlers and also some sawn off deer antlers. The caves are approached by a track starting at a fish-farm (NC 253179) by the roadside several miles south of the Inchnadamph hotel and we give more details on p.88.

Ledmore and Elphin

Ledmore (NC 248125) is a junction where the road from Ullapool (A835) joins the A837 which enters *Suilven's World* from Lairg and the east. Two miles south of this junction on the Ullapool road is the straggling and fertile crofting settlement of Elphin (NC 214114). Elphin is also on limestone and the base-rich soil has a noticeably grassier and greener vegetation than the acidic peatland bogs that dominate the lower-lying parts of *Suilven's World.* There is a small farm open to visitors in the tourist season that specializes in highland animals, including rare breeds such as Soay sheep which roamed StKilda for over 1000 years. There are refreshment facilities and a craftshop nearby.

Just South of Elphin prominent cliffs to the east of the road are the key feature of Knockan Nature Reserve (NC 189092). Now under the auspices of the recently formed Scottish Natural Heritage organization, this is part of the larger Inverpolly National Nature Reserve which takes in Stac Pollaidh (NC 108106), Cul Mor (NC 161119) and Loch Sionascaig (NC 120140), a beautiful island-studded loch that is virtually invisible from any road, but has delighted many hillwalkers as they scan it from nearby hills, including Cul Mor and Stac Pollaidh. There is a low level walk to this loch that we describe in Chapter 3. The Knockan Reserve has both a nature trail (Chapter 7) and a geological trail (Chapter 5).

Further afield

There is a lot to see and do in our *Suilven's World*, and about which we say more in the specialist chapters. But if you make our *World* your base, it is also worth moving further afield. Birdwatchers should make a trip to the sanctuary on Handa Island (NC 135480). A drive further north beyond Kinlochbervie (NC 220566) and Oldshoremore (NC 208586) and then a walk of a few miles leads to one of Britain's finest unspoilt beaches at Sandwood Bay (NC 220655). One may also make a pilgrimage from near Durness by passenger ferry (NC 378661), and thence by four-wheel drive vehicle (or bicycle), to far north-west Cape Wrath (NC 260748).

To the south and east, on the Ullapool to Garve road (A835), Lael Forest (NH 196805) with its several forest walks and a pleasant forest garden with a wide range of labelled specimen trees is worth anything from half an hour to half a day of your time, and near Braemore (NH 209777) some 12 miles from Ullapool, a few minutes may well be spent on the short and easy walk to view the spectacular Corrieshalloch Gorge (NH 203780), a National Trust for Scotland property and famous beauty spot. The falls are spectacular after heavy rain. Many visitors to these parts also make the longer trip to the famous Inverewe Gardens (NG 862819) near Poolewe just north of Gairloch, where the late Osgood Mackenzie raised plants, some sub-tropical, from nearly all parts of the world, to prove just what could be done with intelligent planning in the far north of Scotland. There is a shop where surplus seeds and plants from the garden are often available, as well as the usual range of National Trust for Scotland items. The gardens are one of the Trust's showpiece properties and they doubtless encouraged Robert Irvine in his hydroponicum experiment at Achiltibuie. Where else could one get the inspiration to grow bananas so far north?

3 *Walks on coast and hills*

Our sermon on the mounts

Unless you keep to roads or only to well-maintained stalkers' tracks in the glens, walks, especially on hills or mountains, call for sensible planning if they are to be both safe and enjoyable. Simple precautions may save unneeded misery, or worse, danger. A fickle climate means that a Scottish hill of two or three thousand feet demands the respect reserved for many three times this height in more docile climates.

Even for a one- or two-hour walk on a road or well-constructed path it is wise to carry warm clothing no matter how mild it is when you set out. Take a map, too, for although you are unlikely to become lost on such a walk, a wrong turning may leave you a long slog home or rob you of the enjoyment of the best part of a recommended route.

For tramps in moorland glens or for straightforward hill-walking be sure to

- wear suitable footwear and clothing;
- take sufficient food;
- carry relevant maps, and if needed, an appropriate guide-sheet or guidebook;
- pack a compass (and know how to use it), a whistle and a torch;.
- add a simple first-aid kit.

For major hill-walking or serious mountaineering

- take simple basic survival gear;
- in winter carry an ice-axe and crampons (and be sure you know how to use this equipment);
- leave information about your proposed route and expected latest time of return either where you are staying, with a friend or with the local police; **always confirm** your return as soon as you get back.

for rock climbing add

- ropes, pitons, safety helmet and other rock-climbing equipment.

Important as the equipment itself, is knowing how to use it. A few years ago accidents on Scottish hills and mountains were often due to people being poorly equipped. More recently many of those in trouble have been well clad and fitted out, but have not known how to make best use of their equipment.

But do not let our sermon put you off walking. For the average visitor to the Highlands, unless one engages in rock-climbing or specialized mountaineering, which calls for adequate training, the steps to ensure safety and enjoyment are largely commonsense ones.

Commonsense

First, clothing and footwear. On a fine day it is tempting to set out in T-shirt and shorts — but if you do, take insect repellant and warm, preferably waterproof and windproof, clothing in your pack unless the met office have forecast with complete confidence that the weather will stay fine (and even then you may be misplacing your faith; *Suilven's World* has a climate that is often unnoticed by urban outposts like the Glasgow Weather Centre).

Beating the midges calls for insect repellant, especially if the day stays, or becomes, dull or windless. You may need those extra clothes if there is a sudden weather change. Even if there is a confident and correct forecast of good weather, there is usually a sharp temperature gradient as you climb; that pleasantly cooling breeze at sea-level may contribute a significant chill factor at 3000 feet. Remember, too, if it is sunny, to wear a wide brimmed hat and a long-sleeved shirt or blouse (Plate III); there is minimal filtering of harmful ultraviolet rays at altitude.

Footwear is all-important. In Highland Scotland on all but paved roads ordinary sandals are definitely out. Some specialist firms now make specially designed 'walking sandals' but for most people these are only suitable for well-constructed and well-graded tracks since they give little or no ankle support. Even in the driest of summers, remember too, there are still some boggy moorland areas. Trainers may be adequate for some walks on well made stalking tracks, but even they provide little protection against spraining an ankle. We recommend strong comfortable boots over good thick socks. *Strong* need not equate to *heavy*. Light and flexible, yet strong, boots are available. Some people like green wellies for boggy country. They are water-proof, but we find them uncomfortable, feet becoming warm and sticky, and unless they are a good fit over thick socks they may prove as blister inducing as ill-fitting boots. This is a matter of choice.

On a cool day don chill-proof clothing early, **not** after you become wet or cold. If it gets warmer you can shed a layer. Except in the driest of summers we find gaiters useful when traversing boggy ground. Go for waterproof and chill-proof gear. Various 'breathing' fabrics are ideal. *Gore-Tex* is one well-known trade name for such fabrics, used for jackets, trousers, gaiters and even the uppers of boots. 'Breathing' fabrics, properly maintained, ensure that not only is the rain kept out, but that you do not make yourself even wetter (and sometimes in the long run even colder) by swimming in your own perspiration.

Pack energy-giving and thirst-quenching food — chocolate, raisins and not easily bruised or squashed fruit such as apples, tangarines, clementines, oranges are all good for a day trip, but plums, peaches or grapes usually make a horrible mess in your pack as they disintegrate to a near-inedible pulp. Add biscuits or sandwiches according to your tastes. Carry a little more food than you think you will need in case you are out longer than you expect or somebody has an accident. Some people take cool drinks; some a flask of tea, coffee or soup; others rely on the waters of the many burns and lochans for their liquid refreshment, but there are areas in the Scottish hills where drinking water is not readily available. A can of beer, or a half bottle of chablis may be tempting, but remember that alcohol has a dehydrating effect. You may do better to do your drinking in a pub after your walk.

The key navigational aids are an appropriate map and a compass. The relevant 1:50000 Landranger ordnance survey map is usually adequate. Remember that for **most** of *Suilven's World* this is sheet 15 —*Loch Assynt & surrounding area.* The scale (1.25 in. to 1 mile or 2 cm to 1 km) allows sufficient detail for safe navigation. In fog or mist, your map may be of little use without a compass. Learn how to use that compass before you set out and remember that compass readings may be upset by local magnetic fields, or by proximity to photographic equipment such as automatic exposure meters. Remember too that a compass can only give reliable guidance if you know your precise position when you start using it. So, pin-point your position on the map before the weather clamps down and turn to your compass *before* you get lost.

If you are lost, except perhaps in extreme cold, you are often best to stay put, making use of any available shelter (e.g. a rock or over-hanging tree to protect you from wind or rain). It is for attracting attention in such emergencies, or for an accident such as a broken leg or a twisted ankle, that we recommended that whistle and torch. The former is useful day or night, and the

latter, of course, principally at night. It is a good idea also to wear bright clothing, e.g., some red or yellow item to help location in the event of injury.

If lost in poor weather, hypothermia is a real danger. Much has been written about digging into snow-holes in winter, but preparing one is a skilled business needing appropriate tools such as an ice axe. Without the relevant equipment and the knowhow to use it, keep off the Scottish hills in wintry conditions. We say wintry, rather than winter, deliberately, for these conditions are not uncommon in autumn or spring — and, although only rarely, they may even occur in summer. As a protection generally against cold or shock-induced chill it is wise to carry at all times the simplest of all survival gear — a large black polythene refuse bag. Or better, a bag specifically designed as a survival unit.

The first aid kit need not be elaborate. Assorted adhesive dressings, e.g. Elastoplast, a general purpose bandage and a crêpe bandage are key items. Antihistamine cream is a great comfort if you are particularly sensitive to insect bites or a potential victim of sunburn and standard pain-killing tablets used with discretion may be useful in case of injury or to ease a sun- or wind-induced headache. Safety pins are ideal for securing bandages, or for an emergency repair if you rip your breeks!

If one of your party has an accident and you have to leave them to seek help, if you know your precise position and can pinpoint it on the map, immediately note the grid reference (see Appendix A). It is easier for the police and mountain rescue team, and may save vital minutes or even hours, if you can say you left the victim at grid point (NC 089035) rather than simply 'somewhere on the ridge of Ben Mor Coigach near a big rock'. There are a lot of big rocks like that in Plate III on many mountains.

In the stalking season between about mid-August and mid-October seek permission to enter estate land, and enquire about safe routes on any given day. The best place for advice is usually the local estate office, and addresses and telephone numbers are given in a guide published by the Mountaineering Council of Scotland and the Scottish Landowners' Federation entitled *Heading for the Scottish Hills.* For example, the estate office for the Assynt estate, which includes Glen Canisp and Suilven is centrally situated in Lochinver, the telephone number 01571-844203, but check locally the telephone number of any estate office relevant to a planned walk, for many Highland numbers had been, or were about to be, changed at the time we write. Besides being a potential spoil-sport if you interfere with stalking, high-velocity rifle ammunition may well put a permanent end to your walking and all other activities.

The term 'countryside code' is much bandied about. Most of its recommendations are common sense. If you find a gate closed, leave it that way after you pass through. Do not disturb sheep or cattle unnecessarily. Keep dogs on a lead if this is requested. If in doubt about right of access to land, and the legal situation is complex and not always clear, ask permission or make local enquiries; the aforementioned *Heading for the Scottish Hills* tells

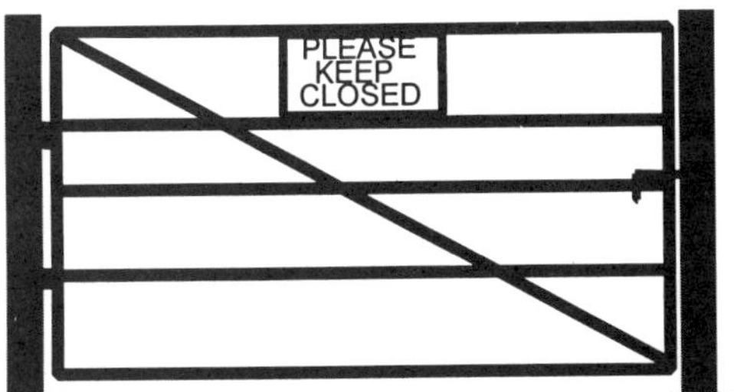

you how to set about this for many estates. As we write there are mounting pressures for clarification of rights of access. When parking at the start of a walk do not obstruct any gateway (even if it looks as though it might not have been used for years) or leave your car where it might hinder traffic, e.g. in a *passing place* on a single track road.

Books on all aspects of Scottish walking are readily available. They range from those covering pleasant hour-long rambles to guides describing the best approaches — either scenically or for ease of walking — on favourite hill or moorland routes, and extend to those detailing challenging mountain or rock climbs.

For serious hill-walking in *Suilven's World* we recommend either the Scottish Mountaineering Club's (SMC) hillwalkers' guide *The Corbetts and Other Scottish Hills,* or Cameron McNeish's *The Corbett Almanac*, but the latter does not cover 'other' hills. Although *Suilven's World* has only two Munros — mountains over 3000 feet — namely, Conival (NC 303194) and Ben More Assynt (NC 319202), there are a number of fine peaks in this category outside the district that are easily reached in day walks from a base in *Suilven's world.* These include the famous An Teallach (NH 069844), a striking landmark to the south of Little Loch Broom and visible from many parts of *Suilven's World*, and often rated Scotland's finest mountain. If you plan any serious Munro climbing we recommend the companions to the above Corbett volumes, *The Munros,* from the SMC, or McNeish's *The Munro Almanac.* Because they are more compact though a little less detailed, some walkers prefer McNeish's books, but it is a matter of personal choice; all four are excellent books compiled by experts..

There are many outstanding coastal and glen walks in the area; some of these are described in a booklet *Making More of Assynt*, published by the Assynt Mountain Rescue team; also local hotels, hostels, many B&B establishments and tourist offices can usually provide information about walks. We give brief notes about a few possible outings in this category in the next section before we turn to more strenuous hill-walks. To give all detail would make a book in itself, so please seek more information from a book about walks, or local sources, as needed.

Some low-level walks

Achiltibuie, Lochinver, Inchnadamph, Achmelvich, Kylesku, Elphin and Ullapool are good bases for low-level, and other, walks of varying difficulty. From whatever base, some walks require, a usually not-too-long, car (or cycle) trip to the ideal starting point.

Two of our favourite shorter walks in the region, each taking a half-day or less, are from Inverkirkaig to the Kirkaig Falls and Fionn Loch, and from Loch Lurgainn to Loch Sionascaig.

Kirkaig falls and Fionn Loch. The Kirkaig Falls trip (Plate I) is probably the most popular walk in *Suilven's World*. A good path starts from the Inverkirkaig bridge car park (NC 086193) and you need no more than strong and reasonably waterproof footwear, the track being muddy in only one or two places during, or after, rain. Signposting at the start is adequate; the path follows the river before climbing at a moderate gradient to give good views of the river below. It is some two miles to the falls (NC 112179) which are not visible, though often audible, from the main track; to reach the falls from here take the right fork at a clear junction. The descent to the river to get the best view of the falls is steep, but not dangerous if you take sensible precautions. The left fork from this junction follows the river a further half mile or more to its source at Fionn Loch (NC 123177), where the reward for your efforts is a fine close-up view of Suilven. This section is often rather wetter than the earlier part. The return journey from carpark to Loch takes about two hours, but allow extra time to admire the falls, and on a fine day to sit by the lochside and perhaps enjoy some chocolate or an orange, but don't forget to take the wrapping or peel back with you for disposal. Would that all walkers would heed the slogan used by the National Parks Authority in antipodean Tasmania:

If you can carry it in you can carry it out.

Loch Sionascaig. The walk from Loch Lurgainn over the low saddle between Cul Beag and Stac Pollaidh to Loch Sionascaig is another popular half-day walk, though less well known than that to the Kirkaig Falls. The track is unsignposted, but clearly marked on the Landranger map. It leaves the Drumrunie-Achiltibuie road some 5 miles from Drumrunie and a few hundred yards before a cottage on the left marked on the map as Linneraineach. The track on the top side of the road starts at (NC 127089) and strikes up the hill through a small group of pines and soon levels out in the saddle between Cul Beag and Stac Pollaidh. About a mile from the start there is a downhill-track to the left at (NC 135101). Beyond the deer-fence just below the turn-off this track continues to the eastern shore of Loch Sionascaig at NC 138118 and the going is reasonably easy, although the path is obscure in places. The map shows the track ending at a bridge across the burn connecting Loch an Doire Dhuibh and Loch Sionascaig. Sadly the bridge (little more than a log with a primitive handrail) was washed away a few years ago. During dry spells it is usually possible to ford this burn with only a small risk of wet feet and to wander through pleasant meadow-like grasses on the other side. Those who are put-off by the vagaries of ill-defined tracks and missing bridges may enjoy an alternative, and some think more enjoyable, walk by ignoring the left branch at NC 135101 and continuing straight on, skirting the lower western flank of Cul Beag to reach a small attractive sandy beach at the eastern end of Loch an Doire Dhuibb (NC 146102) after passing through some attractive birchwoods. Wear stout foot-wear, for the latter part of this track is often boggy in places, though well defined.

Achmelvich to Clachtoll. The cliffs and shore to the north of Achmelvich (NC 057247) are fine areas for rambles. There are various routes, mostly on well-defined and reasonably dry tracks, returning either in the same general direction or else joining the coast road at one of several points between Achmelvich and Clachtoll (NC 042275). Be warned though, that if your car is at Achmelvich, the road is the long way back! In this area, just beyond the ruin of Alt na Bradhan (NC 056259) there is an old meal mill with several mill-wheels and the race providing the water to drive the wheels still visible.

Loch Glendhu. If one crosses the bridge at Kylesku and turns down the dead-end road to Kylestrome (NC 221345), once the route to the old ferry, there is a well-formed stalking track along the north shore of Loch Glendhu. An old croft with stables at Glendhu (NC 284337) near the head of the Loch are used in the stalking season (when permission should be obtained before using the track). The trip to the croft takes a good 2 hours each way, and it is worth following the track a further mile or so up Glen Dubh beyond the head of the Loch, where there are several fine cascading waterfalls on the hills to the south. About 2 miles from Kylestrome, the track passes a small power-station (NC 251342) at the foot of an attractive waterfall on a burn that tumbles into the Loch. This station provides electricity for the Kylestrome Estate. A clear sloping line on the rocky hill on the south side of the Loch highlights a geological feature, the Glencoul thrust, of considerable interest (see Chapter 5, and Plate V).

Achnahaird Bay to Garvie Bay. Another pleasant and easy coastal walk in the Coigach area, although there is no track marked on the map, is from Achnahaird Bay to Garvie Bay. Leave your car in the parking area at the junction of the Achiltibuie and the Reiff Roads (NC 021124) in view of the nearby beach at Achnahaird (Plate II), and walk along the shoreline to the east of Achnahaird Bay, keeping in general to the tops of the low cliffs, although there are easy descents to the water's edge at several points. On the bay to the west of Rubh' a' Choin (NC 033150) you pass a ruined croft (NC 028146) close to the shore. In this bay you have a good chance of being greeted by an inquisitive seal as well as numerous sea-birds, sometimes including eider duck. From Garvie Bay near the river mouth (NC 040137) back to the road (NC 039130) is fairly easy going, though sometimes wet, if you follow (but not too closely) the west bank of the Garvie river. It is a road-walk of nearly two miles back to your car. This trip is in the long half-day category, and despite no tracks being shown on the map, there are many sections where there are well-used paths.

There are several low-level day walks well suited to a two-car arrangement, i.e., two parties leave cars at the opposite ends, and walk to meet mid-way, swapping keys when they meet. You need faith in the other party's ability to drive your car safely to the après-walk rendevous and trust in your and their navigational skills to meet part-way for the key-swap!

Tumore to Loch Nedd via Glen Leireag. A relatively easy walk in this category is that from Tumore on Loch Assynt to Loch Nedd on the coast road from Lochinver to Kylesku. The route starts as a good stalkers' track at Tumore (NC 184267), where it is signposted to Nedd. After a moderate climb for a mile or so, it drops gradually through Gleann Leireag towards Loch Nedd. The route skirts the western flank of Quinag. The latter parts of the track are less clear than the earlier section. In particular, if one starts from Loch Nedd there is no signposting. The track meets the coast road less than a mile on the Kylesku side of Loch Nedd opposite a rectangular and slightly dilapidated concrete tank (NC 156334). A small cairn at the roadside indicates where to cross a burn running parallel to the road to find the start of the track. Return the same way if you have no car swapping arrangement. The return trip takes about 5 hours.

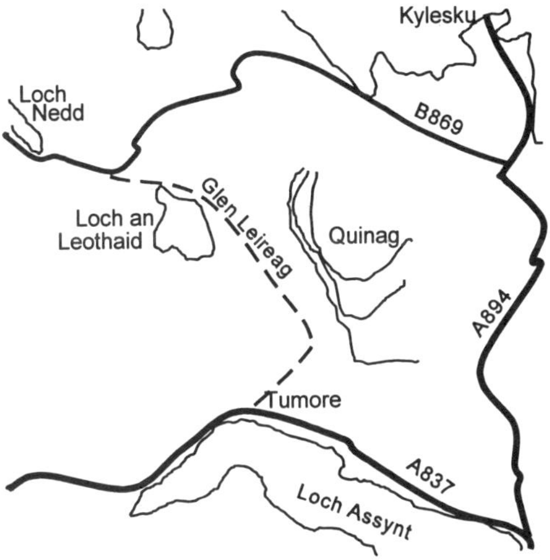

Two longer and tougher walks ideal for car-swapping arrangements are from Lochinver to Elphin via Glen Canisp and the old postie's coastal route to Achiltibuie, from Strath Kanaird to Culnacraig.

Lochinver to Elphin via Glen Canisp. For this walk one follows the stalkers' track (but not in the stalking season without first checking at the Assynt estate office in Lochinver) up Glen Canisp from Glencanisp Lodge (NC 116221) with fine views of Suilven to the right and Canisp to the left. The track is well defined and generally in good condition until one reaches the ridge (NC 215156) beyond Lochan Fada (NC 205165). From this point the track, harder to follow, bears south towards Cam Loch (NC 215135). There is possible confusion because of several tracks in this area not shown on the Landranger map that lead to various small lochans popular with fishermen. However, once Cam Loch is in sight to the south, even if the track is missed it is a not too difficult moorland walk to reach that Loch and pick up the track again on the shoreline. If starting from Elphin similar problems may occur in following the track when it leaves Cam Loch. Careful map reading helps. Allow 5 hours or more for the one-way traverse of this route, which reaches the main road north of Elphin at an unnamed point with grid reference NC 230121.

Achiltibuie to Strath Kanaird. This is a shorter walk than that described above, but it is a route for moderately experienced walkers. Although there has been at least one fatal accident on the route in recent years, it requires reasonable care rather than special skills. At the Culnacraig road end (NC 064040) follow the farm road through the crofts to join the Ullapool track at NC 064034. This track, incidentally, extends westward to the road-end at Achduart (NC 049038), an alternative joining point convenient for those starting from the Achiltibuie Youth Hostel at Acheninver (NC 042057). The track is indicated by marker poles and red paint blobs on rocks though some of these aids are now less distinct than they were a few years ago. Proceeding from Culnacraig, the first hurdle is the Allt nan Colsiche (NC 069032). One has to scramble down a steepish bank, and if the burn is in full spate a dry crossing may prove difficult. Beyond this burn, the track skirts the lower slope of Ben Mor Coigach which here drops steeply to Loch Broom. Heather and bracken on this sector are sometimes thick enough to partially obscure good footholds so care is needed. At the mouth of the Garbh Allt (NC 081026) the track descends steeply to the shoreline; in the pools and under the rocks on the small shingle beach, especially at low tide, there is a range of small marine and shore life. From Culnacraig to here is the more interesting part of the route, so those that have not arranged a car-swap often turn back. Not very distinct markers indicate where the path climbs out of this small bay heading towards Strath Kanaird and it now slowly veers inland with glimpses of Isle Martin off-shore, climbing several hundred feet before Strath Kanaird and the main road north come into view. There is then a gradual descent to the car park at the end of the spur road from Strath Kanaird to Blughasary (NC 135014).

The Rubha Coigeach peninsula. A long, but reasonably easy coastal walk that may be done on either a car swapping or round trip basis is the trek round Rubha Coigeach peninsula from Reiff to Achnahaird bay via the headland at Rubha Coigeach or *vice versa*. This walk is a favourite with bird-watchers or those who hope to spot seals and perhaps dolphins and other marine creatures at play. There is no unique defined path, but various tracks made by humans, or sheep, broadly follow the cliff-tops and coastline. From Reiff (NB 966144) to Rubha Coigeach (NB 981182), the most northerly point on the peninsula, the going is relatively easy and generally not too wet in summer and autumn providing one keeps reasonably near the coast, but above any cliffs. Some of the inland ground on the peninsula across Rubha Mor is very boggy, so it seldom pays to cut corners unless you stick to relatively high ground. You may well see seals at play off the coast and especially in the main bays between Reiff and Rubha Coigeach. The coast from Rubha Coigeach to Achnahaird gives fine views north to Stoer lighthouse and inland to the mountains of Assynt and Coigach. The cliffs in many places are thronged by sea-birds, in the spring many nesting on rocky ledges. Seals and eider duck swim in the bays below the cliffs. There are several easy and obvious descents to the shoreline, but in general follow the clifftops. The road is reached at Achnahaird bay car park (NC 016140). The coast route is some 10 miles, but if you are not on a two-car expedition the road walk back to Reiff via Altandhu adds another 4 miles on reasonably easy gradients.

Eas a' Chual Aluinn. A more strenuous low level walk is to the waterfall, Eas a' Chual Aluinn. The track is well defined except for the last half-mile or so to the falls, but involves quite a bit of ascending and descending. The starting point is on the A894 between Skiag Bridge and Kylesku. A track leaves this road at NC 238284 heading eastward and skirts the south shore of the nearby Loch na Gainmhich. We prefer this to a less distinct track, also shown on the map, to the north of the Loch, leaving the road at NC 240292. The track branches near a burn at NC 273278. Here take the fork that follows the left bank of the burn first north then east to the top of the falls (NC 280277). Walk carefully on the cliff tops beyond the falls to find a vantage point to see the Maiden's Tresses (p. 34) at their best. There are some accessible terraces on the cliff face that give good views, but keep within your walking or climbing abilities.

Tralligill. There are some interesting walks to various caves in the Inchnadamph area. Because of its archaeological interest, we describe that to the 'Bone Caves' at Allt nan Uamh in Chapter 6, p. 88. Other pleasant rambles start by the farm road (NC 250218) a few hundred yards north of Inchnadamph hotel and proceed by the stalkers' track up the River Tralligill into the Inchnadamph Nature Reserve in Gleann Dubh. There are a number of underground caves in this area, e.g. at NC 276206. About one mile of underground passages has been explored, but the caves should only be entered by experienced and properly equipped cave explorers and potholers. This is an interesting area in which to study the vagaries of underground rivers and burns.

Hill and mountain walks

You may be surprised that we are not giving very precise details for specific hill walks in *Suilven's World.* We love hill walking, but it is a more serious business than glen or coastal walking and detailed information on the *best* way to tackle any hill is a prerequisite for an enjoyable outing. Such detail is readily available in the Corbett or Munro guides produced by the SMC which we referred to earlier, or in Cameron McNeish's *Corbett Almanac* or the companion *Munro Almanac.* Choice of a relevant general guide is a matter of taste. There are also good descriptions in other books such as W.A. Poucher's classic *The Scottish Peaks* or the local *Making More of Assynt* published by the Assynt Mountain Rescue team. The SMC also provides numerous books for the serious mountain or rock climber covering all areas of Scotland. New books on various Scottish walks appear every year, appealing to a variety of tastes and covering routes suitable for all categories of walkers from first-time venturers to those who are interested only in the more difficult rock climbs. Hotel proprietors and local residents are also often able to give advice on specific walks.

Please, please, plan your hillwalking carefully with the aid of maps, books or local information, so that you minimise the prospects of having to call out the rescue services. It is because of the space needed to give precise details for each walk, and the ready availability of that information elsewhere, that we give only outlines here. We try to say enough about each walk to help you select ones that you feel might be appropriate to your experience of, and inclinations about, hill-walking. We cover only a few of our favourites.

For many hills and mountains there is more than one approved or regularly-used route to the summit. In general, we mention only the more direct and safer routes. These would usually be spurned by determined and enthusiastic mountaineers or rock climbers.

Stac Pollaidh (NC 108106). This is the most climbed mountain in Coigach and Assynt. Many people believe the erosion problem caused by walking boots is so great that it would be wise to ban climbing the Stac for some years. Even if such a ban were practical it is doubtful whether 'recovery' would take place without additional measures. In 1993 limited work was done on a shoe-string budget to stem the worst effects of erosion, but the problem will only be tackled successfully by building a costly stepped *erosion-proof* path to the top. Such an engineering project itself might produce scars nearly as unattractive as the present erosion. The cure could be worse than the disease! It has been argued that climbers should not make frontal attacks on the last steep sector to the ridge, but that all should use the track that skirts the eastern flank and make the final ascent from the back of this mountain in minature. Those who know the Stac are aware of erosion problems on the north-facing slope as well, although these are not clearly visible from any road.

The challenge presented by the Stac stems from isolation, combined with the impression it gives of being bigger and more difficult to climb than it really is. For the fit, the direct ascent from the car-park (NC 108095) above Loch Lurgainn to the ridge takes only about an hour. Although there are many difficult-to-climb pinnacles on the ridge, these may be dodged by taking one of a number of avoiding paths. Only a small percentage of those who attain the ridge actually go to the highest point, which is at the western end. To reach this one has to surmount a guardian rock just short of that summit. There are good footholds, but this is a dangerous manoeuvre for the inexperienced, especially if you have no head for heights. Do not attempt this last bit if you have any doubts. The fine all-round views from the Stac are there for the taking without attaining those last few feet to the highest point.

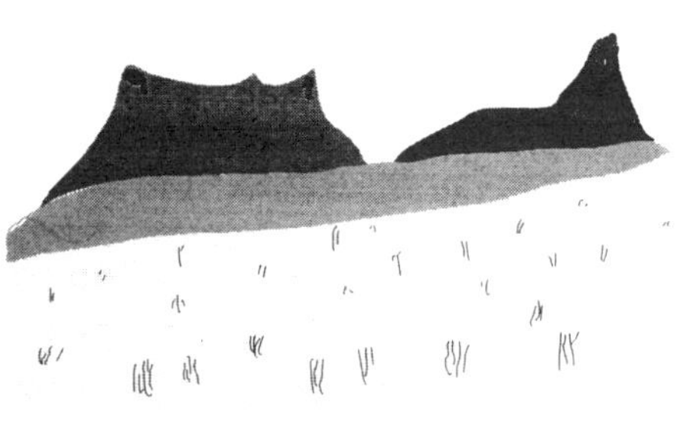

The Coigach Hills. These hills rise behind Achiltibuie and the best known summits are Ben Mor Coigach (NC 095043) and Sguirr an Fhidhleir (The Fiddler) (NC 095055). There are about as many suggested routes on these hills as there are guide books. Viewed from Drumrunie or Loch Lurgainn the Fiddler looks a considerable challenge, yet from Culnacraig (NC 065040) the ascent, after a moderately steep but by-no-means-formidable climb from the road, degenerates into an almost boring trudge to what seems from that approach little more than a bump on the horizon. It is worth that slog to reach the top for the superb views across to Beinn an Eoin (NC 105064), Cul Beag (NC 140088), Cul Mor (NC 161119) and Stac Pollaidh (NC 108106). Golden eagles may sometimes be seen soaring around the cliffs on the Fiddler's steep northern face.

Ben Mor Coigach is often approached either as a second leg after taking the easy route to the Fiddler, or by a long slog from Drumrunie. If the weather is not too windy (when this part of the route should not be attempted), the interesting part of the Coigach summit is the ridge of Gharb Choireachen (NC 084035) with its superb views of Ullapool and Loch Broom and the mountains beyond. There is a good path along this narrow ridge and down the steep descent towards Loch Broom as far as a band of scree some half way down where, when descending, it is wise to turn sharp right to cross the Allt nan Colsiche near the point (NC 080041), below which that burn tumbles into a steep gorge. From here head for Culnacraig, although there is no obvious track. An enjoyable day may be spent taking in not only these but some of the lesser Coigach peaks such as Cairn Conmheall (NC 065055) and Beinn nan Caorach (NC 079053).

Cul Beag (NC 140088). A popular route to this mountain is from the track to Loch Sionascaig that we described in the previous section on p.46. On reaching the low saddle (NC 128094) above the small pine cluster some half mile from the starting point at the road (NC 127089), bear uphill and then cross towards the small but distinct 'Pap' (NC 140093) aiming at the col between this and the main peak. From there it is a steep but straightforward scramble to the top. One may return by the same route, but a pleasant alternative is to head south-eastward, then south, to rejoin the Achiltibuie Road, but take care to avoid the cliffs running in a general southerly direction from the summit. A longer but gentler route to the summit is over the slopes from Drumrunie (NC 166054). There are possible ascent routes on the northern face, but even the easiest of these is best left to experienced hill-walkers well versed in map-reading as a number of small cliffs are best avoided.

Cul Mor (NC 162119). The easiest route to Cul Mor starts on a stalkers' track to the left of the main road (NC 189095) just beyond the Knockan Visitors Centre when travelling towards Elphin from Drumrunie. The track peters out after a couple of miles but stone cairns mark the route onto Meallan Diomhain (NC 171117). Of the two peaks of Cul Mor, the more westerly is the higher. Opinion is divided as to whether it is better to ascend this directly by its northeastern flank, or whether one should make for the gap between the two peaks. Both summit peaks are worth ascending, and for one of the finest views of Loch Sionascaig and its islands we suggest you add the easy walk out to the cliff tops on Sron Gharbh (NC 153125).

Suilven (NC 153184). After Stac Pollaidh, Suilven and Quinag are probably the most climbed mountains in *Suilven's World*. Suilven's highest point is on the western buttress of Caisteal Laith and Suilven would probably be even more popular than either the Stac or Quinag were it not that any route requires a trek of 4 to 5 miles from a road-end before the ascent-proper begins. There is little to choose between the two usual routes, that from Inverkirkaig car-park (NC 086193) near Achins bookshop, or that up Glen Canisp from Glencanisp Lodge (NC 116221). Whichever you choose, there is a steep climb to the Bealach Mor (NC 157182) between the western rounded Caisteal Laith, the summit peak, and the middle peak, Meall Mheadonach (NC 161179). An unexpected feature on the ridge just west of the Bealach is a fine drystone wall of uncertain purpose and origin. The track passes though a gap in the wall (where there was doubtless once a gate) and unless you have a poor head for heights there is little difficulty in reaching the summit of Caisteal Laith from where one has an all-round view of *Suilven's World* — the inspiration, we feel sure for the title of a popular guide to Assynt — *Land of Rocks and Lochs*. As Caisteal Laith is surrounded by cliffs — indeed one suggestion is that the origins of the wall may have been to prevent sheep wandering onto this danger zone — you should return by the recognised path to the Bealach. Do not attempt to climb Meall Mheadonach or the more easterly Meall Beag (NC 165178) unless you have some basic rock-climbing experience and a good head for heights. For those able to arrange a car swap the ascent can be made with one party starting from each of Glencanisp Lodge or Inverkirkaig, and returning to the other. When doing a return trip to the same starting point, we find the Glen Canisp route marginally easier. If you start from Inverkirkaig, opinion is divided as to whether it is best to proceed along the stalkers' track to a point NC 144168 before ascending to the Bealach, or whether one should cut across the higher moorland roughly on a line from NC 132180 to NC 153177. Scattered cairns mark possible routes approximately on this line, but some people find these confusing rather than helpful.

Canisp (NC 203187). Some hillwalkers think Canisp is an uninteresting mountain. This is unfair. To be sure, the usual route from the northern end of Loch Awe (NC 248159) a couple of miles north of Ledmore junction, and up the long but steady incline to the summit may be a tedious and seemingly long two-hours-plus climb, particularly on a hot day, but the views from the top, especially that of Suilven on the opposite side of Glen Canisp are as spectacular as one might expect from a fairly isolated peak. The route takes advantage of the non-steep face of Canisp, and especially to the west and southwest there are some fine cliffs and steep slopes.

Quinag (NC 209292) rivals Suilven for popularity among hill-walkers. It is a three-spur range and all the main peaks can be climbed in one day if you are fit. The usual starting point is near the highest point on the A894 between Skiag Bridge and Kylesku. There is ample car parking in a small gravel quarry (NC 232274) on the right when heading north. A stalkers' track on the oppsite side of the road leads further than shown on the map and almost to a point north abeam the sometimes forbidding-looking Lochan Bealach Cornaidh (NC209282) tucked under the steep cliffs of Spidean Coinich (NC 206277). Sail Garbh (NC 209292), the highest point, is on one's right and it is a reasonably easy ascent from the end of the stalkers' track to the bealach or saddle (NC 200285) between Spidean and Sail Garbh and a not too difficult climb from this bealach to the Sail Garbh Ridge. Some prefer the steeper, but not dangerous, climb direct to the ridge from abeam the lochan. One may also climb Spidean Coinich from the bealach, but the going is steep and the route is best avoided in strong winds as there are one or two almost knife-edge sectors on the ridge.

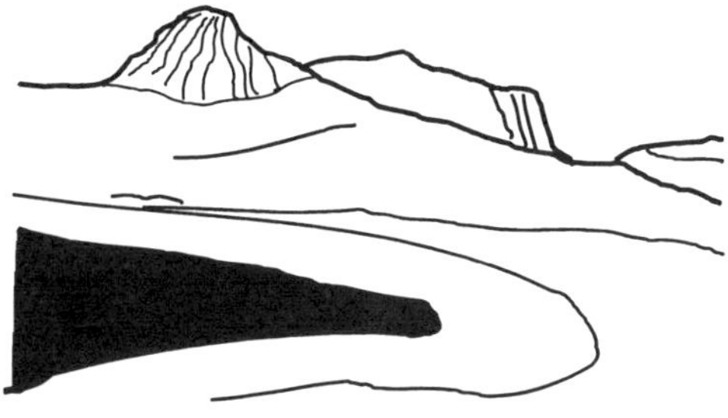

If you want to climb all main peaks of Quinag, it is better to leave the stalkers' track about half a mile from the road at NC 227276 and strike left up the slabbed slope towards Spidean Coinach. Only the last sector to the top of Spidean is steep, but even this is not forbiddingly so. One then proceeds (providing the wind is not too strong) over several smaller peaks and down the steep descent to the bealach, next ascending to a small peak shown at a spot height of 745 m (NC 201289), but unnamed on the Landranger map. That ascent is not as difficult as it looks from below. From the spot-height point follow the long ridge walk via one subsidiary peak to Sail Gorm (NC 199304), the north-west spur of Quinag. From here return nearly to the 745 m spot height and strike across to Sail Garbh. It is worth — if time permits — continuing past the trig cairn at the summit to the end of the ridge (NC 213298) for a fine view of Kylesku, the bridge, and the surrounding lochs. The return may be made by backtracking and striking down to the stalkers' track near the Lochan from a point on the ridge between the trig cairn and the 745 m. spot height. Choose a point nearer the latter if you want to avoid too steep a scramble.

An alternative route to the Bealach a Chornaidh (NC 200285) on Quinag is from Tumore (NC 185267) on Loch Assynt, following the Loch Nedd track (p.48) until opposite the Bealach, then striking up the steep slope to the Bealach. Despite its steepness, this is the shortest route to that saddle.

Conival (NC 305198) *and Ben More Assynt* (NC 319202). These are the two Munros in *Suilven's World.* Ben More Assynt fails by only 2 metres to reach the 1000m mark. It and Conival are conveniently both climbed in one trip. The starting point is the farm road (NC 250218) just beyond Inchnadamph Hotel. It is a long walk and the target mountain is not visible for much of the distance, so it is important to follow guide book directions. In good weather the ascent by the usually recommended route is not difficult or dangerous, but care is needed in windy weather or in fog; in the latter it is easy to strike out on an incorrect ridge between the peaks. The best views from Ben More Assynt are those to the north, although vistas in other directions open out at several intermediate points. An amusing account of this walk is given by TV personality Muriel Gray in her book *The First Fifty*.

There are many other coast, glen or hill walks within *Suilven's World*, including fine cliff walks, for example, in the Stoer and Drumbeg areas, and although it does not look impressive from below, Glas Bheinn (NC 255265) is higher than Suilven, being a Corbett, though by no means so striking a mountain. It is an easy though steepish climb via its north-western slope. Breabag (NC 293180) is another Corbett not to be despised.

There is a near endless list of possible walks not far outside *Suilven's World*. A favourite of ours is Ben Stack (NC 270422) which has many of Stac Pollaidh's 'mountain in miniature' features. Munros which we have tackled on day trips from a base in *Suilven's World*, but which are situated outside it, include Ben Hope (NC 478502), Scotland's most northerly Munro. An Teallach (NH 069844) is arguably Scotland's finest mountain, but the ridge traverse is not for the faint-hearted, and has potential dangers if a route is not carefully matched to one's experience and skills. The ascent of Beinn Dearg (NH 259812), a long but not difficult slog, is rewarded by fine views from the top. The Fannichs are a group of hills including Sgurr nan Clach Geala (NH 184715). Although less spectacular than An Teallach or Beinn Dearg, the Fannichs provide good hill walking with nine tops in the Munro category.

Details of these and many other walks are included in the guides we have already mentioned.

4 *The story of the people*

The myth of timelessness

In our opening chapter we exploded the myth that the Western Highlands have existed almost unchanged not only for decades, but even for centuries or millennia. Indeed, currently well established practices such as crofting that are indisputably a unique feature of Highland lifestyle are comparatively modern. Land tenure systems and rights, first implicit and later legal, have changed dramatically since the era of clan battles in and before the turbulent days of the massacre of Glencoe. The clan structure itself was unknown to the earlier Picts although they in turn had a more organized social system than that of the first nomadic wanderers.

Even newer lifestyles like crofting have themselves changed dramatically within little more than two centuries. Many early crofters shared their home with their cattle and their hens. A peat fire was kept burning at all times, the smoke escaping only through a hole in the roof, and this fire was the centre-piece of the living room. In those days crofters had no security of tenure, occupying their holdings on little more than a grace and favour basis.

It is true that the Highland economy and lifestyle have developed differently from that of the rest of Britain. This, in part at least is because until comparatively recently there was only minimal direct communication with the rest of the UK. Isolation gave rise to a time warp in a sense we described in Chapter 1, but that is not the same as time standing still.

Many of the first crofters descended from an earlier group of 'clansmen' who were not themselves blood members of the clan they served, but soldiers and followers of the clan chief, who in those days was a true leader and organiser rather than the modern figure-head who provides little more than a focal point for what are often diffuse bonds of kinship. The much-talked-about 'clearances' of a now seemingly under-populated Highlands were in part a hamfisted response to a problem of over-population in a changing economic climate. Throughout history lifestyles have had to adapt to changes in land usage and productivity, some man induced, others the whims of nature.

Because extensive written records of Highland events have only existed for a few centuries there are many perhaps mythical, and certainly over-simplified, explanations for some of the changes. About 11 000 years ago the last ice-age in *Suilven's World* came to an end. For some 3 million years before that the area had experienced a succession of ice ages with coverings of ice-sheets and a build-up of glaciers. The exposed barren rocks left by the last ice-cap as it gradually receded, eroded further to add soil to that already brought down by glaciers, and these initially barren soils became colonized by plants of ever increasing complexity, eventually leading to a suitable habitat first for animals and eventually for humans. Some 5000 years after the last ice-cap had melted the lower ground was covered in forests largely of Scots pine and birch, perhaps also hollies, rowans and alders. Oaks were common further south, but although present, were perhaps less widely distributed in Assynt and Coigach; we say more about forests in Chapter 7.

Early days

Some 8000 years ago, perhaps even a little earlier, Scotland's first settlers, nomadic tribes, wandered in the developing forests and along the coasts, hunting and fishing. They did not cultivate the land. The little we know about these early arrivals comes from archaeological studies that have unearthed accumulations of bones and shells, largely remains of fish, birds and small animals that were probably snared or killed with stones or primitive weapons. The most important discoveries of this kind in *Suilven's World* were made early this century in the Allt nan Uamh caves (NC 268170). These indicated that men lived in those caves — sometimes known as the *Bone Caves* — and also that the caves might have sheltered species of animals such as lynx and bears now long extinct in Scotland. Human presence was first confirmed by signs of fire and the unearthing of deer antlers that had clearly been cut by crude tools. It is likely too that some of the animal remains found were brought there by primitive settlers as part of their larder stock.

About 3500 BC — again the date is only approximate — agriculture came to the Highlands; hunting and fishing as ways of providing food, then being supplemented, or partly replaced, by growing crops and keeping livestock. The origins of these first 'farmers' is uncertain, but there is some evidence from the position of stone monuments that they might have come up the straths and glens from the east probably at a time when the climate was warmer than it is today. Primitive agriculture involved some clearing of forests, but it was not until about 2000 BC that a change to a colder and wetter climate triggered a major decline in the forests, a decline that was to continue for several thousand years. This nature-induced deforestation was accelerated by firing and cutting to provide timber for building and fuel. Clearing of forests may also have been speeded by a deliberate policy of reducing woodland because it provided shelter for wolves, foxes and other predators on farm stock. At later dates the Vikings doubtless took some of the remaining timber for ship-building. Also in parts of Scotland, though we believe mostly in districts further south, a great deal of wood, especially oak, was cut for conversion to charcoal for iron-ore smelting. The deterioration of the forests when the climate became cooler resulted in once-fertile soils being covered in a layer of acidic peat that eventually developed to the peat bogs and heath moors with us today. But we digress, for we cover the land and its plants in Chapter 7. Our immediate interest is in how the economic consequences of these changes interacted with the lifestyles of the people.

In the immediate pre-Christian and early-Christian era the inhabitants of northern Scotland were the Picts, the name believed by some to mean the *'painted people'*, but only after the Roman invasion of Britain are there records and description of these early settlers. The origin of the Picts is obscure, but they certainly practised, and perhaps even brought, agriculture to Scotland. It is not clear whether the settlers from the east coast mentioned above were Picts, and it has been suggested that some Picts may have come from continental Europe and settled in the west, rather than the east of Scotland because of the more sheltered harbours and better-developed forests. We find historical accounts vague on this point.

In *Suilven's World,* as in many other places, it is likely that there was some overlap between the stone, bronze and iron ages. The still-fertile soils associated with the limestone base around Inchnadamph were certainly settled throughout these periods. The evidence already mentioned from the bone caves for early nomadic settlement was followed by discoveries of the remains of crude stone memorial cairns and burial chambers as well as by finding bronze axes and a number of stone round-houses, all of which are later developments indicating continuing settlement. Chambered tombs probably date back as far as the fourth millennium BC although their use extended over several millennia. Of the several in the Inchnadamph–Elphin area a well-known example, described in Chapter 6, p.93, (see also Plate VIII) is that near Altnacealgach (NC 262112) about 1¼ miles east of Ledmore Junction on the road (A837) from there to Lairg and Bonar Bridge.

These early settlers thought their dead more worthy of lasting edifices than the living, their homes are believed to have been cruder shelters constructed from leaf, bark and tree limbs.

Chambered tombs and memorial cairns predate fortified settlments of a type found throughout Scotland. These duns, or forts, were not so much military strongholds as we know them today, but were rather defensive settlements in which the community lived, or could retreat to if attacked..

The most substantial and best known Pictish fortifications or dwellings, the round brochs, usually had only one, often narrow and low, entrance. This made it easy to ambush an unwanted intruder. Potential intruders may have at first been rival 'tribes' of Picts, but the many coastal duns suggest also a fear of invasion from the sea. We have no reliable information as to when domination of the Picts by Gaelic-speaking Scots, who moved north from the 5th century onward, took place in Coigach and Assynt. It was probably a gradual transition. The Gaels migrated from Ireland to Argyll bringing with them Celtic Christianity, and their penetration north is thought to have been largely by land.

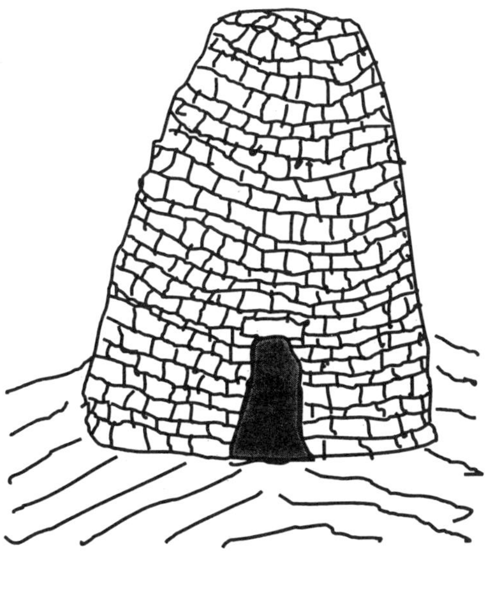

The first direct sea invaders of *Suilven's World* in the Christian era were the Vikings, towards the end of the eighth century. Their influence in this mainland sector of the Highlands was not as strong as it was in Orkney, Shetland, Caithness and the Western Isles, although there were Viking settlements on the Summer Isles and probably a few coastal mainland settlements. Their language did not replace, or even strongly influence Gaelic, as the dominant language, although some place names have Viking origins, e.g. Sutherland was the Viking 'Southland' and Suilven itself is commonly interpreted as a hybrid Viking—Gaelic combination of the Viking 'Suil' (or 'Sula') and a probable corruption 'ven' of the Gaelic 'beinn', the whole translatable as *The Pillar Mountain*. Even if not an overtly inspiring name, this, surely, is more appropriate than the senseless or misleading designation 'Scotland's Matterhorn' used in at least one tourist guide.

The clans

In the 11th century the clan system became widely established. The clans in Coigach and Assynt were at first closely tied to those of the Western Isles, and their fortunes and vicissitudes, like those of the entire clan system, have been closely linked to the machinations, clan feuding, and wider conflicts that culminated in the Jacobite risings. A preponderance of MacLeods and MacKenzies in Coigach and Assynt arose from and developed during turbulent and sometimes bitter struggles in the Highlands that started some 800 years ago. Early in that period Assynt was, for about a century, in the hands of the MacNicols of Lewis before passing, at first peacefully through marriage, to the MacLeods of Harris. The MacLeods had Viking origins. The mechanics of how the MacLeods of Harris gained official title to the lands of Assynt in the 14th century is vague, but grants of

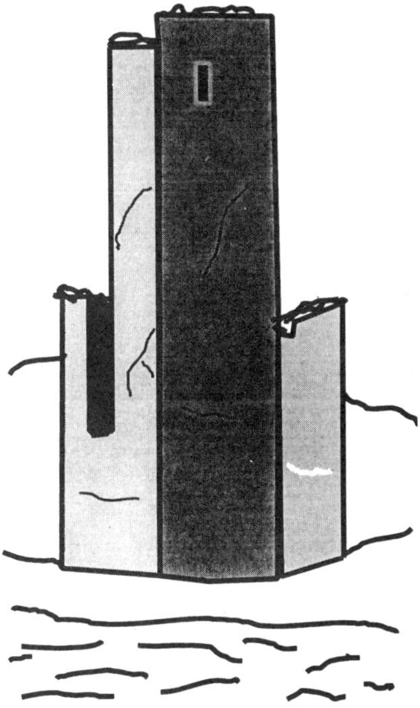

land to West Highland chieftains were at that time often little more than bribes from the Scottish Crown to secure allegiance during the wars of Independence. In the fifteenth century a MacLeod became the first MacLeod of Assynt in his own right. Ardvreck Castle, (NC 240237), now only a prominent but crumbling ruin on the eastern shore of Loch Assynt became the 16th century stronghold of the MacLeods.

The clan story in Assynt then took on complexities and improbabilities worthy of a Mozart opera. The Assynt MacLeods, though technically now a clan in its own right, was only a small one, and got drawn into quarrels involving not only the MacLeods of Lewis (who appear by unspecified means to have banished the MacNicols) but also into the affairs of the Earls of Sutherland and Caithness and the Mackays. The MacKenzies, a catholic clan, ousted the protestant MacLeods from Lewis and claimed a right to Assynt. The then head of the MacLeods was outlawed as a 'lawless Highlander' accused of brutal murders. He avoided capture with some help from the Earl of Sutherland who was keen to keep the MacKenzies out of

Assynt. This did not stop the MacKenzies raiding Assynt and carrying off livestock and burning houses, although in Coigach the clans seem to have got on rather better in their relationships, for in 1612 Margaret MacLeod married Rory MacKenzie and the two names are still common in Coigach. In 1650, Neil MacLeod of Assynt backed the wrong side when he captured the defeated Royalist Commander, the Marquis of Montrose, and imprisoned him in Ardvreck Castle. The Marquis was later taken to Edinburgh and executed. Neil MacLeod paid for this 'treason' on the restoration of a Royalist Government with a term of imprisonment, and the estates fell into debt.

According to Malcolm Bangor-Jones in *Land of Rocks and Lochs*, the MacKenzies invaded Assynt in 1672, capturing Ardvreck Castle. At about the same time Assynt was acquired by the Earl of Seaforth's family and he installed the MacKenzies as tenants. The MacKenzies proved poor estate managers and later fell out with the Earl of Seaforth who was by then in dispute with the Duke of Sutherland over the Assynt Estate. The bankrupt holdings were sold to the Sutherland estates in the 1750s.

Despite the clan rivalries and wider disputes in that turbulent period, Assynt and Coigach, our *Suilven's World,* were winning fame for, and acquiring considerable wealth from, their Highland cattle, although all farms also grew crops — especially oats and barley. The larger farmers prospered not only from ownership of land and cattle, but by leasing grazing.

Although the crofting system as we know it today has clearly -defined origins dating back only some 200 years, events that led to its establishment had their roots in the feudal system of landholding established in the 11th and 12th century, an era which, in Scotland, saw a transition from what might be regarded effectively as tribal communities, to one where large grants of land were made to individuals, often for services rendered to king or country, and sometimes land was given also to incomers to the Highlands. Thus a system of established, even though not legally formalised, tribal rights gave way to a new framework of landowners' rights. The Scottish kings increasingly exercised a right to grant land for services rendered. These services often included the provision by a clan chief of fighting men or equipment such as boats. Clan chiefs needed not only their kinsmen, but also other followers to help with tasks on the land and to provide fighting men both to be put at the disposal of the king or perhaps to take part in inter-clan disputes or battles. In return for such duties these *clansmen*, as they were called, were usually given a shelter, often primitive, and perhaps a small piece of land on which to grow crops or to keep sufficient cattle to provide them and their family with milk, butter and cheese, also one or two sheep to provide wool which the clanswomen made into cloth. As this system evolved there was no fixed tenure of their land, and indeed the clansmen were often moved from place to place according to the needs of the clan chief. There was no legal framework governing the relationship between the clan chief and his kin to the clansmen. The system worked on a basis of good faith on both sides.

It was as agricultural methods improved that the Highlands became famous as a breeding region for cattle. The lands from Knockan to Inchnadamph, with their limestone soils provided excellent grazing. Increasing numbers of cattle called for better organization, so relatives — and sometimes friends — of the clan chief, known as tacksmen, became responsible as tenants for farm operations over whole areas. Tacksmen were an extra layer —

somewhat akin to today's middle managers — in the then-existing social structure and each clansman was allocated to a particular tacksman and, in their role as workers, the clansmen were provided with primitive homes and given a small strip of land to work, together with some common grazing rights, in return for a 'rent' payable in the form of carrying out farm work for the tacksman. Failure to do this occasionally lead to a clansman being dispossessed of his home. This appears to have happened only rarely, and probably only with some justification, until some greedier tacksmen starting demanding monetary rent as well, and then woe betide any clansman who could not, or would not, pay this. These increasingly formal arrangements between tacksmen and clansmen gave no legal protection to the latter.

After Culloden

The system we have just outlined, so far as we can ascertain, worked without drastic problems until the disastrous Jacobite uprising in 1745. The defeat of the Jacobite forces at Culloden in 1746 brought a fundamental change to the Highland way of life. Improved communications began to erode the isolation of the region. The clan system was weakened politically and militarily by the disastrous outcome of the '45. Clan chiefs began to spend more of their time away from the Highlands, and adopted a new lowland, or even English, life-style — a style that called for more money, and the chiefs looked for better returns from their estates. The once thriving cattle market was no longer producing enough profit. There were two potential sources of extra revenue. The first was a growing demand for alginate, extracted from kelp, and then widely used in the manufacture of glass and soap. The second was to introduce the new tougher breeds of sheep that could graze successfully on the course vegetation and stand the rigorous Highland climate. The first of these was labour intensive, but essentially a sea-shore activity, and hitherto most of the clansmen in Assynt lived and worked in the agriculturally richer inland. By contrast, sheep grazing required less labour than the cattle raising it was gradually replacing.

As an inducement both to the clansmen and to incomers needed for alginate extraction, landlords offered small pieces of land near the coast and a share in common grazing in return for work at a minimal wage in the kelp industry. This was the true birth of crofting. The work was hard and exhausting, but proved profitable to the landlords, especially during the Napoleonic wars, but the trade collapsed afterwards. The potential for commercial fishing was also recognised about this time, with fishing stations being set up at Lochinver, on Tanera Mor, on Isle Martin and later at Ullapool, but the industry could barely support the numbers that had been brought into the area by the 'kelp' boom. The last straw was the rapid development of the sheep industry with its minimal need for labour. The Highlands suddenly became 'overpopulated' in an economic sense in that there were not the jobs to support the population. With varying degrees of ruthlessness, Highland landlords, some themselves recent incomers, banished the remaining 'clansmen' from the glens to an inhospitable and already over-crowded coast, often on terms and conditions that meant virtual starvation. Crofters were actively encouraged to emigrate and some were given varying, but usually meagre, assistance to do so. Others had no option but to emigrate on being thrown out of their crofts (from the Gaelic *coirtean*, meaning a small enclosed field) for failure to pay rent. It is a moot point whether the clearances were acts of sheer malevolence or sometimes a genuine but pathetically inadequate attempt to provide opportunities for what in the 1990s we call redundant employees. Even if not malevolent, the policy was carried out with scant evidence of benevolence, and it has left bitter feelings to this day.

Clearing the glens to make way for sheep began in Assynt in 1812, some 160 families being banished to an already crowded coast which could not provide them with a decent living in the following decade. Several hundred left *Suilven's World* for Nova Scotia, New South Wales, Van Diemen's Land and other young colonies between 1775 and 1840, but this did not relieve the poverty for those left behind, for the available land was still overcrowded.

The crofting story

In 1846 the potato crop failed, triggering a crisis which at least drew public attention to the plight of the crofer. A board was set up to relieve the situation by providing food and work, largely in the form of road-building — constructing what were called the 'destitution' roads. Some local estates also tried to provide work and food or to assist further emigration. However, the root cause of the problem — people having not enough land to provide a living, and no security of tenure — was not then tackled.

There are several excellent histories of crofting, we list two in the Further Reading section and although both deal with the problem as it affected the Highlands and Islands as a whole, much of what is said applies to *Suilven's World*. The system was a closely knit one and its survival through times of adversity owes much to the willing help that crofters gave one another.

The church, government authorities, the legal system, all had a role, often ignominious, in the saga. Feeling among crofters that the established Church of Scotland sided with the landlords accounts for the rapid growth and large following of the Calvanistic Free Church. Psychologists no doubt have explanations as to why this hellfire and damnation cult first obtained, and has continued to exert, so firm a grip on Highland life. The God-fearing influence of this church on people's outlooks is evident in the inscription on a tombstone in the Badenscallie Burial Ground (NC 036061) near Achiltibuie. The stone records the death of a three-year-old child and adds:

> *His favourite expressions were 'Jesus will put his good spirits in baby's heart', 'Nice Jesus' and 'Baby will love Jesus when he gets to Heaven'.*

The child was the son of the then Coigach Free Church minister. Some hundred years after that inscription was cut into the stone, it will strike many people as 'over the top', but it accurately reflects the all-consuming obsession with religion at that time, for it provided a beacon of hope for the future in what was, for many, a soul-destroying present.

Law officers, landlords' agents and policemen trying to evict crofters in the mid-nineteenth century often had their authorization papers taken and farm buildings were set alight by disgruntled crofters. An Act passed in 1886 gave crofters security of tenure and a right to fair rents. As so often when politicians try to sort out a mess in a way that they hope will placate everybody, they succeeded in pleasing nobody. Landlords complained that the act gave too much to crofters, the crofters that it did not go far enough.

In 1911 the Crofters' Commission was given powers to arbitrate in cases of alleged injustice. Between the First and Second World War there was some tinkering with the legislation that affected crofters, and stronger action came in 1956 when a new Crofters' Commission was set up under an act passed the previous year with wide powers for supervising the whole crofting system, including the reletting of vacant crofts, allocation of common grazing rights, and financial aid to crofters.

Under the 1976 Crofting Reform (Scotland) Act a crofter was given the right to buy his croft and certain associated lands at a price related in a specific way to the rent. Welcome as this reform was, it still failed to take full account of the fact that the crofts were often too small to provide a living. Indeed, from its very beginning it had never been intended that a croft should provide a full living, but what changed dramatically at or about the time of the clearances was that the crofters no longer worked for a landlord so they had to look for other sources of supplementary income.

For the last 100 years crofters have sought ways to increase their income. There has been a decided, if at times erratic or faltering, increase in the opportunities for them to supplement the inadequate living possible from the croft. The late Victorian era saw the development of sporting estates that provided employment in the appropriate seasons as stalkers or gillies. An expanding tourist industry has provided part-time employment in hotels and also work in the building trades as facilities for visitors have been extended and up-dated. The Forestry Commission in its schemes to rejuvenate the forests — even if not in the form of the historic Caledonian pine forests — has provided another pool of employment, as have developments supported by the Highlands and Islands Development Board (founded in 1966) and more recently by European Community money.

While parliament has not seen fit to accept crofters' claims for the return of the land to the people, an event took place in *Suilven's World* in 1992 that opened a route for crofters to achieve this goal. On 8 December 1992 the Assynt Crofters Trust purchased the North Lochinver Estate, and it has pioneered a system in which all crofters have equal voting rights in the running of the Estate. It is early days to assess the viability and durability of this move, but it has received a warm welcome from the Highland community at large and from well-wishers further afield. At least one similar scheme is being explored in a Hebridean island as we write. The move has challenged what some see as an inevitable trend for ownership of large estates to pass to absentee landlords not only from England, but also from continental Europe and the Middle and Far East.

The population decline in the Highlands that started with the clearances has now been halted, even reversed by developments in the tourist industry and an influx of retired people from other parts of Britain. These changes are a mixed blessing. They have brought more jobs but they have increased pressures on the housing market, often putting property prices beyond the means of potential local buyers. The influx of retired people, has also underlined the trend towards an aging population. Increasing demand for holiday homes, these often occupied for only a few weeks each year, has also put pressures on the housing supply.

Myths and legends

Because written records are often sketchy, it is not surprising that there is a rich vein of folk tales in *Suilven's World.* We mentioned on p.12 a possible derivation of the name Achiltibuie as *The Field of the Yellow Boy*, but we have been unable to find out whether the boy and his brothers of that local legend were Vikings or earlier nomadic settlers.

In *Land of Rocks and Lochs*, Kenny Mackenzie — a name to affirm local ties — gives a selection of Assynt folk tales, some with clear associations with the imbibing of 'a not-too-wee dram', others referring to local landmarks said to induce strange behaviour in animals or people, while some are tales of Scottish guile, or just pleasant flights of fancy. Many of the 'old hands' of *Suilven's World* are good sources of such tales, and happy to tell them. Some of the stories improve in the telling after the narrator has taken a wee dram.

5 *The story of the rocks*

A geologist's paradise

It is common in *Suilven's World*, especially during University vacations, to find a group of students chipping away with geological hammers at a road-side rock cutting or at a remote hillside outrcrop. They will have chosen Assynt or a nearby part of Sutherland for this exercise because it contains not only some of the oldest rock on earth, but also because the overall rock structure is fascinating.

In the foreword to his excellent *Highland Landforms,* Robert J Price wrote of these formations:

> *They can delight the eye as a part of landscape, infuriate the engineer or planner, be a challenge to the mountaineer or a series of problems in the mind of the earth scientist.*

Our planet is some 4500 million years old, and the oldest rock formations in the Highlands were laid down between 1000 and 3000 million years ago, indeed recent researches have hinted that some may have been laid down even a few million years earlier. In the previous chapter we saw that humans first settled in Western Scotland about 8000 years ago. It is not easy to relate our familiar biological time scales for human events to those used by geologists. It helps if we construct a scaled *time map* somewhat analogous to the geographer's space map. We do this by squeezing the 4500 million years since the planet was created as a fiery inferno up to the present time into a mapped period of just one 24-hour day. On this time map, if we take midnight to mark the creation of our planet, then the following midnight represents the present time. On that scale the last 8000 years, the entire period humans have been in Scotland, corresponds to about the final one sixth of a second before the terminal midnight. A human life-span of 80 years corresponds to 1/600 of a second. There was a series of ice ages lasting some 3 million years just before humans came, and these had a major influence in sculpturing our landscape. On our telescoped time scaled, these 3 million years reduce to less than the last minute of the 24 hours. If we assume that many of the oldest rocks in the Highlands, these some of the oldest rocks on earth, were laid down about 3000 million years ago that corresponds to about 8 a.m. on our 24-hour time map.

A good place for the novice to get a feel for the geology of *Suilven's World* is at Knockan cliff (NC 189092) just a mile or so south of Elphin. The Knockan Reserve is an extension of the Inverpolly Nature Reserve, managed for many years by the UK Nature Conservancy, but now under the control of the recently-formed Scottish Natural Heritage.

Knockan has both a nature trail and a geological trail and guide pamphlets to each may be obtained for a nominal fee at the visitors' centre. The parking area and the trails are open all year, but the centre is attended only during summer months. Please heed the request not to collect specimens, and to leave geological hammers in your car. In this chapter we describe some features of the geological trail.

The international fame of Knockan arises from a geological anomaly that was first explained here; similar formations have now been discovered on every continent. Before describing this particular phenomenon, we say something about the general geological structure of the area and explain how the rock formation has influenced the scenery and landscape.

Its geological history explains why the northwest coast of Scotland, unlike the east coast, has many deep fjord-like sea inlets, also why most of these are aligned from sea entrance to headwater in a generally northwest to southeast direction. It explains why the mountains of the region are predominantly isolated peaks rather than extensive ranges, and why this mountain structure is not repeated in the Eastern Highlands. It also accounts, in part, for why much of the area is either peatland bog or bare rock, and why certain areas, for instance around Inchnadamph, Elphin and near Ullapool have a generally lusher, greener vegetation.

In one short chapter we cannot give explanations for all these outcomes, but we look now at key events in the geological saga of the region. Normally rock is deposited in layers of various ages, the oldest at the bottom. These layers undergo numerous contortions during the millions of years of geological time, sometimes tilting, sometimes being submerged beneath the sea, or spewed forth from the ocean bed as the result of volcanic activity or subterranean upheavals. In recent geological time (towards the present-day midnight on our 24 hour map) the rocks of Assynt and Coigach have been subjected to further erosion by

- ice and glacial action,
- running water,
- wind,
- waves.

In Assynt, the bottom layer, called Lewisian gneiss, is the oldest rock found in Britain. This grey rock, complex in structure, was formed between 1 and 3 thousand million years ago by recrystallization of even older rocks. The name 'Lewisian' comes from the island of Lewis, where the rock is also found. Modern geological evidence suggests that this rock was laid down when Assynt and the rest of the Northwestern highlands lay at the south-east corner of a continent that included both north-east Canada and present-day Greenland. At Knockan the gneiss is below the surface, but in the Lochinver area, the many rocky knolls, so characteristic of the landscape on all roads out of the settlement, consist of gneiss. The hardness of this stone makes it ideal for road building. It does not break down readily, but where it does, it gives rise to acid infertile soils.

Some 800 million years ago the gneiss was covered by a layer of the oldest sedimentary rock found in Britain, Torridonian sandstone. This brown or pinkish brown rock was carried down from huge mountains probably in an area near where the Outer Hebrides are today by east-flowing rivers to cover a, then probably submerged, Assynt to a depth of thousands of feet. Glacial and other erosive action has worn away nearly all of this layer except for scattered tougher patches. These 'relics' are Suilven and the other isolated peaks of *Suilven's World* — Quinag, Cul Mor, Cul Beag, Stac Pollaidh, Ben Mor Coigach. The coastal cliffs at Stoer Point and elsewhere on the Sutherland coast, are also of Torridonian sandstone. Weathering has resulted in a series of ledges that has made the cliffs round Stoer (NC 021356), and those further north at Handa Island (NC 135480), ideal nesting place for sea-birds.

The shape of the land, the pattern of lochs and rocks, has been greatly influenced by those several ice ages during the last 3 million years, though many other things happened before that. There is some evidence that prior to these ice-ages the climate might have been warm and much of the area semi-desert. Because of the importance of ice ages, let us digress from the historical sequence to explain why these occurred and how the resulting glaciers so greatly influenced the shaping of the present-day landscape in the geologically short timespan of 3 million years (one minute on our 24 hour clock map).

How do ice-ages develop? Permanent ice-covers form only when the temperature drops sufficiently to preclude the melting of one winter's snow before the following year's fall adds to it. About 3 million years ago a climatic change gave a lowering of temperature sufficient for this to happen. This temperature change probably resulted from some volcanic or subterranean upheaval that triggered changes in the earth's orientation or atmosphere that cooled the north European land masses — a sort of 'instantaneous' greenhouse effect in reverse. After some years of cold, when the ice sheet is of sufficient depth, glaciers are formed and their slow movement causes erosion on a massive scale, forming the cirques, glacial moraines and scoured out valley lochs we see today. Erosion is not directly a consequence of moving ice itself, for as we all know ice produces little friction, but the scouring is caused by the debris of loose stones that the ice collects, giving the base of the glacier a sandpaper-like surface that tears away and traps further rocks as it moves. In this way many (relatively) softer rocks are scoured out and carried away. Much of the Torridonian sandstone and some of the later-formed rocks we describe below are in that category. Only harder lumps of the sandstone, like Suilven, have been left behind.

The jump from a landscape with a Torridonian sandstone thousands of feet deep to one where all but a few peaks and coastal deposits of this stone remain was interspersed by other events. About 600 million years ago the Torridonian sandstone of Assynt, while still submerged beneath the sea, was covered with deposits of white or silvery-grey quartzite to thicknesses usually less than 100 metres. Some mountains such as Cul Mor (NC 162119) and Canisp(NC 204187), more particularly on their eastern slopes have screes composed of quartzite which has been broken down by the action of frost. On others such as Suilven, the quartzite, apart from a few scattered fragments, has almost completely disappeared as a result of ice action. By contrast, Glas Bheinn (NC 255265) has a top largely composed of quartzite, and from this mountain one gets a panorama of similarly topped hills if one looks inland from Inchnadamph in the general direction of Ben More Assynt (NC 318202). Even at lower levels screes of quartzite are visible. There is one on the right of the main road just after passing the Knockan cliffs when travelling towards

Plate I - Kirkaig Falls in full spate, 2 October 1994.

Plate II - Achnahaird Beach on a calm day.

Plate III
A safari hat and a long-sleeved jacket protect against ultra-violet rays and wind as well as against midges.

Plate IV - The trig cairn on Cul Mor.
No longer needed for cartography, these cairns are still a hill walker's favoured goal.

Plate V - Beinn Aird da Loch and the Glencoul Thrust from the A894 near Newton.

Plate VI - Seeding cotton grass enlivens the bogland scene in summer.

Plate VII - Eye-catching lichens on a coastal rock near Reiff.

Plate VIII - Lichens, moss and bracken have invaded the ancient Altncealgach chambered cairn

Elphin. Because of geological upheavals boundaries between different rock types are seldom horizontal, but are tilted at varying angles. This is clear, for example, in our simplified sketch of a cross section from north-west to southeast through Canisp.

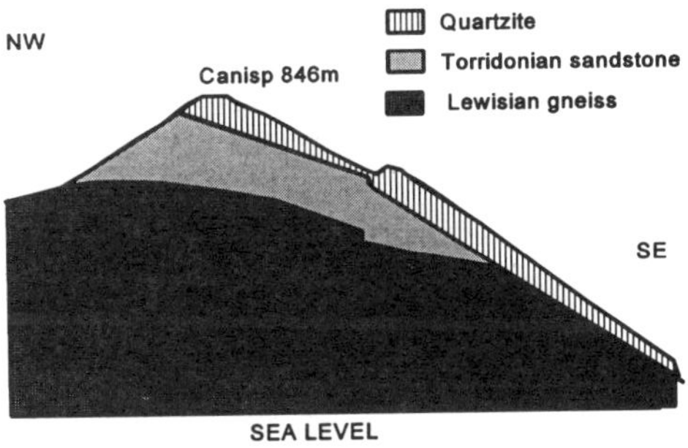

There are several further and younger layers that can still be seen at Knockan. Above the quartzite, and also formed when the land was beneath the sea, is the pipe rock. It resembles the quartzite, but gets its name from the fossilized pipes which run through it; these are burrows made by marine sandworms on the sea-floor between 800 and 600 million years ago, providing the proof that this layer was laid down beneath the ocean. Throughout the Coigach area there is evidence in the hills of what must once have been shorelines at several levels, further indicating how much of the land was progressively thrown up from the ocean, or that there have been changes in sea level. Indeed, the latter almost certainly took place in the various ice ages, the sea-level dropping as each ice-cap on land grew, then rising again as the ice melted between succesive ice ages. The sandworm burrows in the pipe rock represent the earliest evidence of animal life found in the Knockan area, although in other parts of the region there is some evidence of primitive algal life-forms in the Torridonian sandstone.

At Knockan there is also a relatively thin layer of brown shale called the fucoid beds because fossils in them were once thought to be seaweeds, and also a layer of gritty quartzite. Both contain fossil evidence of early marine organisms. Above this is the thicker layer of Durness limestone, young as rocks go, laid down some 500 million year ago when the region was still beneath the sea, but now a transparent sea, inhabited by a number of marine animal species. Fossilized remains of some of these have been found in various parts of the North-west Highlands. Where the limestone layer still exists, as in the Elphin and Inchnadamph areas, there are not only caves but rich fertile limestone soils. How green is the grass at Elphin!

The Knockan Cliffs Reserve holds examples of all these rock types, although because it is underground there, samples of gneiss have been brought in from near Inverkirkaig and incorporated in the trail-laying. But what about that intriguing anomaly that gives Knockan its special place in geological history?

The Moine thrust

Commonsense tells us to expect older rocks to form the bottom layer of a sequence, and that is what we have described so far in our account of the rock formation in *Suilven's World.* Glacial and other erosive actions explain why some layers are missing or are only represented by isolated mountains, or at specific points.

Before we describe the anomaly we need to explain another feature of rock formation. This is that older rocks show more signs than newer ones of, often somewhat chaotic, alterations brought about by raised temperatures and pressure changes while they are buried beneath the newer rocks above.

Now, at the Knockan cliffs there is a top layer we have not yet mentioned; it consists of what are called Moine schists; they are dark coloured banded rocks often broken into slabs. These show evidence of being subjected to high temperatures and pressures while buried under other layers, suggesting they are relatively old. Yet their position as a top layer suggests they are the latest rocks to be formed. These same rocks are of a type found further east, where they are regarded as a base layer in much the same way as is the Lewisian gneiss in *Suilven's World*.

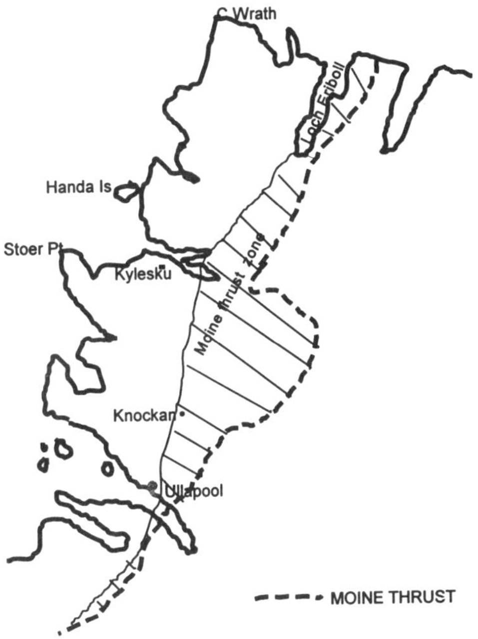

One hundred years ago geologists tended to ignore the contradiction implicit in these rocks being a top layer, and yet showing evidence of early formation. The same situation exists not only at the Knockan cliffs, but on a strip west of a line that extends roughly from the A'Mhoine area east of Loch Eriboll (NC 450620) to the south of the Isle of Skye. Prominent geologists, including Sir Roderick Murchison, a noted Easter Ross geologist and a founder of the Geological Survey, and others, believed that despite the contradiction, because it was the top layer, this rock must be the newest.

It was soon realised that this view ignored the fact that these rocks had a more eventful geological history than the unaltered fossilized sediments on top of which they lay at Knockan.

An alternative hypothesis was put forward by geologists who disagreed with Murchison and his followers. This was that the top and more altered layer of Moine schists was explained by a 'fault', or break in the earth's crust. They argued that pressures or movements beneath the surface, or collisions between continents not only caused these cracks in the earth's surface, but that they allowed these older rocks, probably formed about the time of the Torridonian sandstone or even earlier, to push through the fault to be deposited on top of the newer sediments by 'flowing' over the newer rocks on one side of the fault-line. The validity of this hypothesis was contested by some of Murchison's supporters, but they finally conceded in 1884, and in an article in the journal *Nature* in 1885 entitled *The Highland Controversy in British Geology*, C Lapworth laid the Murchison argument to rest. This important hypothesis, stimulated by the Knockan observation, was the first evidence that faults in the earth's surface allowed forces in the molten interior of our planet or continental collisions, to push older, much altered, rocks to the surface and deposit them on top of newer formations.

These upheavals are now recognised world-wide, many having taken place at different times in geological history and attributable to several different causes, and some of the earlier upheavals even giving rise to great mountain chains. This classic discovery of the phenomenon and the subsequent explanation is associated with the Knockan cliffs. The fault line is at the eastern boundary of the thrust, and the Moine schists were pushed westward from that line on top of the other layers, to form the **Moine Thrust**. 'Moine' is a modification of A'Mhoine, the name of the area at the northern end of the thrust. The great importance of these discoveries in northwest Scotland is explained fully in a famous Memoir of the Geological Survey of Great Britain published in 1907 under the title *The Geological Structure of the North-West Highlands of Scotland.* There are six named authors, the two best known of those being B N Peach and J Horne; geologists renowned for their work in Assynt early this century. The memoir is a geological classic.

Near the head of Loch Assynt, close to the road, not far north of the Inchnadamph Hotel, but on a hillock on the opposite side, there is a memorial cairn erected in 1930 to John Horne and Benjamin Peach, the inscription reading:

> *To Ben N Peach and John Horne who played the foremost part in unravelling the geological structure of the North-west Highlands, 1883–1897. An International tribute. Erected 1930.*

That the tribute is embossed on a metal plate rather than being inscribed in stone perhaps reflects geologists' concern about the erosive effect of the elements on rock, something very evident on headstones in older local burial grounds in *Suilven's World*, like that at Badenscallie (NC-037061).

There are other geological faults and thrusts in the area, some giving the layperson even clearer visual evidence of what has occurred. The most noteworthy and striking of these is the Glencoul thrust (Plate V) which is clearly visible from the A894 as it descends from the saddle between Quinag (NC209292) and Glas Bheinn (NC 255265) towards Kylesku. Here, at a turn-off signposted Newton (NC 234316) if one looks in an east-north-easterly direction at the slopes of Beinn Aird da Loch (NC 282317) on the far side of Loch Glencoul from the road, one sees a sloping shelf which descends from an altitude of some 650 feet at its western extremity (NC 261324) almost to sea-level towards the south eastern end of the loch. Below this shelf are prominent cliffs of quartzite resting on Lewisian gneiss. The rock of Beinn Aird da Loch above the sloping shelf is also Lewisian gneiss which has been thrust westward over the quartzite. This contrasts with the Moine thrust, where the overlying layer consists of Moine schists. The Moine thrust zone does not extend quite so far east as this, but the very top of the Stack of Glencoul (NC 291286), clearly visible as a somewhat drunken-looking cone from Unapool (NC 237328), when looking directly up Loch Glencoul, is in the Moine thrust zone, and is composed of Moine schists.

Ben More Assynt and the surrounding mountains have a complicated fault history and this explains why their structure contrasts with the isolated ice-erosion-formed mountains such as Suilven or Stac Pollaidh.

Our brief account of the geology of the area is superficial, and we give references in our Further Reading list for those who want to delve more fully into this fascinating story. In particular, we recommend Chapter 15 of J N Whittow's *Geology and Scenery in Scotland* for a more detailed, but not too technical account of the geology of the Northern Highlands and how it fits into the more general context of the geology of the rest of the country If we have inspired you to look more closely at the complex geology of this area, then the inexpensive folding pamphlet by D R Shelley entitled *Assynt Geological Motor Trail* is a guide that cannot be bettered, giving a quite detailed account of important features and many of the complexities we have only hinted at, and doing this without getting lost in technical jargon. With the aid of many photographs and diagrams, it tells you just what to look for, and where to find it.

6 *Archaeology — ancient and modern*

Man and his rocks

The Oxford Dictionary defines archaeology as *the systematic description or study of human antiquities, especially as revealed by excavation.* We shall be less formal and interpret the definition broadly, taking excavation to mean not only 'digging' in the sense of removing soil, but to include 'digging out' information about antiquities from reference sources. We also put a loose meaning on 'antiquities' so as to include not only artefacts from ancient times but items, some not very old, which have passed out of current use. This lets us say something about comparatively recent changes in Highland activities and social patterns as reflected by deserted buildings and other remnants. We might describe this by the seemingly contradictory phrase *modern archaeology.*

To learn more about what ancient stones once used by man can tell us about the early settlement of *Suilven's World* read Cathy Dagg's *Prehistoric Loch Broom & Assynt.* It is an informative guide to local sites and explains how they help us build a picture of life in prehistoric times.

As we indicated in Chapter 4, the early nomadic inhabitants of *Suilven's World*, because they had only primitive tools, lived mostly in caves or used only fallen timber, bark and other plant material to provide some form of shelter, so no tangible evidence remains, or could be expected to remain, of such man-made structures. It is only in caves, or from middens of discarded fish-shells near the shore that we find physical evidence of early man's lifestyle and movements.

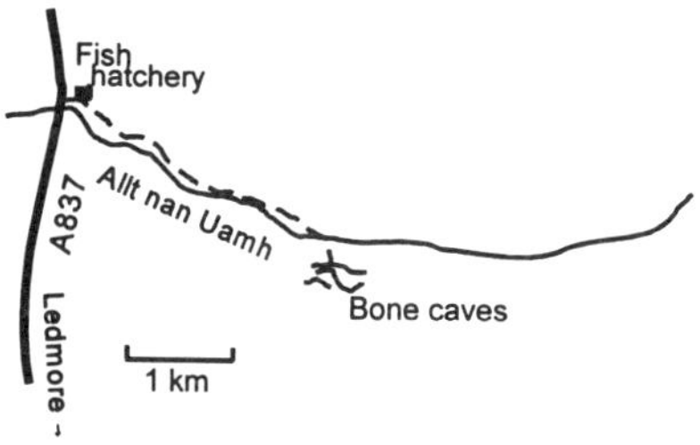

The Allt nan Uamh caves (NC 268170) approached by a path from the salmon hatchery (NC 253178) several miles north of Ledmore on the main road, the A837 have, as we mentioned in Chapter 4, yielded relics of human occupation dating back perhaps to 8000 BC, including bones of species of animals such as the brown bear, lynx, and lemming long extinct in Scotland. At various point on the coast, such as near Achnahaird Bay, middens of fish-shells indicate the feeding grounds of tribes or groups, even though no visible remains of buildings or belongings such as weapons, tools or ornaments have been found at most of these spots.

Prehistoric settlements

The durability of stone means that there is lasting evidence of how the next wave of primitive humans used it first to build symbolic monuments to worship the sun, moon or other gods or for burial of their dead, and only later for shelters for themselves.

Such remains require more digging out in the literal sense than does evidence of the immediate past, such as the ravages of depopulation as reflected in the many ruined houses — stark windowless, doorless, roofless dwellings that were, often less than a century ago, family homes echoing to the laughter of children. There are remnants too of pioneering efforts of past centuries such as old droving roads once used to take Highland cattle to market, or to transport quarried rock, but which are no longer in use today and discernable only as scars on the landscape.

Hints of where there may be buried tombs, fortifications or other buildings may be as obvious as a formal irregularity in the land often having a defined, if imperfect, general shape, e.g. a raised or sunken circle, or a broadly rectangular pattern with clearly elevated lines indicating the position of walls, or depressions corresponding to rooms, chambers or passageways. There are less obvious signs of ancient constructions, some visible only in aerial photographs taken under the right conditions. These include patterned changes in growth of crops or in the natural flora corresponding to position of stoneworks, ancient drainage channels, or lands once farmed or cropped over considerable periods. Such artefacts still affect present-day plant growth even though the changes they cause are not visible at close quarters to the naked eye, or if they are, it may not be obvious at ground level that they form a pattern.

The early monuments and burial chambers were often incorporated with or took the form of stone cairns, and there are many of the latter in *Suilven's World,* although we know of no evidence in the Assynt or Coigach districts of standing stones like those at Callanish on the Isle of Lewis.

Monuments and burial chambers date from around 4000 BC. Large blocks of stone were used in their construction if these were available locally, but if not, best use was made of smaller local stone. The tombs were mostly communal burial chambers and were generally in use for many years, certainly for several centuries. In these parts of Scotland the passage-grave construction appears to have been more common than the gallery grave. The former was basically a circular chamber entered by a passage and placed within a round cairn, the latter usually a rectangular chamber under a rectangular cairn. With many chambered cairns there is evidence either of extensions to provide extra burial space, or of adornments added at some later stage to basically simple chambered tombs to make them, in the eyes of the then still living, more fitting memorials to the departed. Pottery and other artefacts, assumed to have belonged to the deceased, have been found in a few such tombs. Radio-carbon dating has been used to indicate the relative age of many such artefacts, but unfortunately it is only recently that even moderately reliable methods of linking precise calendar dates to radio-carbon dating have been developed, but technology for doing this is expanding rapidly.

The next use of stone by man was for building fortified settlements, often on hills or headlands and these somewhat loosely built 'tribal' reserves were followed by more formally fortified living arrangements of the dun and broch type. These developments took place over a period from about the first millennium BC to the early Christian era. Exact dating is difficult, for it is likely that progress was not at a uniform pace throughout Scotland or even within the Highlands. Parallel to these developments, and running probably from about 600 BC to the coming of the Vikings more than 1000 years later, was the use of circular huts, their positions indicated now by 'hut circles', especially in Coigach. These round huts had low stone walls and probably timbered roofs with surrounding agricultural land. They lacked the fortification element of duns and brochs. The implication is that they were built at times, or at sites where, the inhabitants were not, or felt they were not, liable to attack from hostile forces.

Hill forts and fortified settlements, unlike our present day concept of a fort as a defence manned entirely by military personnel, were basically defended settlements or villages. Cathy Dagg suggests that some of them may not have been permanently inhabited, but used as places of refuge in the event of attack. The main purpose of the defences was to keep out would-be but unwelcome new arrivals, or perhaps sometimes predators or raiders from similar nearby settlements.

Some remnants from this era show signs of stone dwellings within the outer walls; where there are no such indications it is likely that timber framed domestic dwellings were used, for it was an era when much of *Suilven's World* was still forest. Some fortlike settlements were on hills or coastal headlands, positions dictated by a need to be watchful for potential invaders either from land or sea. Others were on sloping or even flat ground with good agricultural potential, and in these the military defences were often less obvious. Remains of such settlements are usually fragmentary, partly because of natural decay processes, but more commonly because stone has clearly been removed and used elsewhere. The casual observer often finds it hard to tell whether some obviously man-created collection of stones was put in place a thousand or more years ago or just one or two hundred years past. Archaeological skills, however, have enabled a lot of detective work to be done to give pictures of the original structures and some idea of when they were erected. For example, the position of timber posts or stockades is often indicated by shallow grooves or holes in stone walls; breaks in a wall may indicate the position of wooden gates or doors. Walls were often thick, or else there were double walls with the intervening space filled with rubble. Socket holes in such walls indicate where timber beams were inserted.

Evidence that many stone and timbered structures were sometimes set on fire, either accidentally, or by invaders, comes from vitrification, or a fusion of partly melted stone caused by intense heat generated by the fires. Richard Feacham in his *Guide to Prehistoric Scotland* points out that often the vitrification occurs in the vicinity of gates, suggesting that these may have been set on fire by attackers.

The Pictish broch, perhaps the best-known and most distinctive of all early dwellings, belong to a relatively short period immediately prior to and during the early Christian era and many examples are found in the Highlands and Northern and

Western Isles, one of the better known and most easily seen in Sutherland, although not in *Suilven's World,* is the Dundornadilla broch (NC 456449) north west of Altnaharra and just south of Ben Hope. These, usually circular, structures were sometimes 40 feet high, though most were probably only about 20 feet. The walls were drystone structures up to 15 feet thick and the internal diameter was usually between 30 and 40 feet. They had only one narrow low entrance. Better preserved brochs suggest that many had galleries serviced by internal staircases. They were often built on fertile land and one is tempted to draw a somewhat tenuous, but obvious, analogy to a beehive; these were basic settlements from which the workers emerged to till the land.

The Gaelic word *dun* means a fort or fortified dwelling place and in that sense may be thought to include the earlier hill forts already described. However, these predated the Celts arrival and the word dun is usually applied to a later and more formal structure. Galleried duns are usually circular, or oval, with walls up to 16 feet thick. The walls themselves often contained passages and galleries and there were usually steps to the top either within the wall itself or on the interior. The interior enclosure was often 50 feet or more in diameter and dwellings inside were often of timber, or may even have been primitive tents; today the only indicators that they were used as dwellings is often ash remnants in what appear to have been hearths. Duns are also found as coastal fortifications on promontories with the main wall on the landward side and lesser walls defending the steeper cliff faces. There is a wide range of duns, some simple in construction and fairly small, others larger and resembling the earlier hill forts.

We list below some of the places where remains of stone buildings of various types may be found in this region. More detailed descriptions are given for many of them in Richard Feacham's guide or in Cathy Dagg's book, both included in our further reading list. All but a few are clearly marked on sheet 15 of the 1:50000 Landranger map at the given grid reference. If you visit any of these sites please do not remove, mark or disturb the remains in any way. Some show all-too-obvious evidence of past tampering, ranging from removal of stone for use elsewhere to blatant vandalism.

Altnacealgach chambered cairn (NC 262112) (and others). Altnacealgach is the best known of the remains of several chambered cairns in the Glen Oykel area. The main chambered cairn may disappoint the non-expert. One has to be close to it even to locate it. Despite having reasonable instructions on its location (it is marked on the OS sheet 15) it took us some 20 minutes to find it. It is some 200 yards from the A837 a little more than 1 mile east of Ledmore Junction — thus near what we regard as the edge of *Suilven's World*. There is a small cairn, somewhat flat and little more than an elevated mound of stones on the Loch shore; this cairn is also marked on the OS map at NC 260111. It is best to park a car near this, then walk some 150 yards along the road towards Lairg. At that point, strike left up the hill towards a post on the electricity transmission line, then proceed a similar distance uphill from this post to a rounded elevation on the hillside. This is the chambered cairn. It could have been built about 4000 BC. The remains consist of this stony

mound, the lichen covered rock now somewhat overgrown with bracken and mosses (Plate VIII). The main chamber is constructed of large stone slabs, the interspaces being filled with drystone walling. The blocked entrance faces approximately ESE. There is a recess in one corner that is roofed by overlapping slabs.

Many other chambered cairns in the vicinity are marked on the Landranger map south of Ledmore junction in the Elphin region at NC 205105 and at NC 238121 and north of Ledmore at NC 248140 There is also a chambered cairn (NC 241237) near Ardvreck castle and one further north near Scourie (NC 167429). Many more cairns in the Ledmore region are included in a sketch map, and grid references to some given in an appendix, to Dagg's book; in particular, there are several in Glen Oykel, some relevant grid references being NC 298084, NC 303079 and NC 300103.

Inverpolly fort (NC 066155). Situated on a north facing headland that is almost isolated at high tide some half mile north of Inverpolly Lodge, at least one guidebook suggests the best approach to this fort is by boat. Dagg, however, gives instructions for an approach on foot. The main enclosure wall of this relatively small fort is vitrified, probably, as we have suggested above, as a result of the firing of timbered parts of the structure at some stage and the stone being melted by the heat generated. Vitrified ruins on the west coast are more usual further south. The fort is of a type common in the first millennium BC and in the early Christian era.

Dun Canna fort (NC 111008). This fairly extensive fort defends a narrow promontory on a shore a mile or so north of the mouth of the river Kanaird. It is approachable by track from the road-end at Blughasary. It is larger than Inverpolly fort, probably dating from a similar era, although there is evidence that some sections were built later than others.

Culkein fort (NC 041340) is on a high rocky point on the Stoer peninsula beyond the road end at Culkein. The approach is by a moorland walk. A wall some 7 feet thick, built of large stone blocks, crosses the headland to enclose an area that is further divided into two by a chasm crossed by a narrow bridge of rock.

Clachtoll broch (NC 036278). Also referred to sometimes as *Stoer broch,* this probably dates, like most brochs, from the early Christian era or a little earlier and although much of the outer walls have now collapsed it has the typical circular shape of a broch and was probably some 60 feet in external diameter at the base, the double walls being some 15 feet thick. The top diameter would have been about half the base diameter. The entrance in the east, with its triangular lintel, is still discernable.

Strath Kanaird dun (NC 166020) is approached by a moorland walk and is on a rocky knoll between two burns that are unnamed on the map. Probably of Celtic origin, it is thick walled, and D shaped, rather than the circular shape of a broch or some other duns.

Loch Ardbhair dun (NC 168332). This is the ruin of a coastal fortification on a tidal rock at the south end of a small loch below the coast road between Nedd and the junction with the main road south of Kylesku. Unlike Strath Kanaird dun, it is circular.

Clashnessie dun (NC 055315). This dun is not marked on the OS sheet 15 but is a typical promontory dun lying on an almost isolated pillar of rock near the end of a farm road on the western side of Clashnessie Bay. There are the remains of a narrow wall that borders the rock to enclose an area of some 800 square feet.

Achiltibuie hut circles. Flat circles on the hillside at several points on the coastal hills between Achiltibuie and Culnacraig indicate sites of hut circles. These are not shown on the Landranger sheet 15 map, but grid references to the main ones are given by Cathy Dagg. Many are clusters of 3 or 4 circles indicating small communities living peacefully with no evidence of fortifications. As we indicated on p.90 such settlements may date back to 600 BC or they may belong to the early Christian era. There are at least five groupings on the hill about one mile north-east of Achiltibuie. Grid references given by Dagg for some of these are NC 030 089, NC 032 088 and NC 031 085, but none has been excavated. Most are near the burn that flows into Badentarbet Bay at the western end of Achiltibuie. Dagg lists other circles at Badenscallie, (NC 035 064) Achnacarinan (NC 046 048) and Culnacraig (NC 065 033). In the Achiltibuie area there are also built-over remains of what was probably a broch at Achlochan (NC 028 069).

Early Christianity and the coming of the clans

As we mentioned in Chapter 4 the Celts crossed from Ireland to southwest Scotland about the 5th century AD. There is little information on when the Gaelic culture that the Celts brought with them spread north to displace a predominantly Pictic culture. Viking raiders came in the 8th century, although as we pointed out in Chapter 4, their influence in *Suilven's World* appears to have been less marked than in Orkney or in the Western Isles.

By the 11th century the system seems to have stabilized somewhat with Gaelic as the dominant language and the clan system becoming established. The clan groups and their followers probably occupied some of the earlier fortified settle-ments, but a system evolved with clan strongholds or castles appearing, while no doubt the clansmen occupied more modest dwellings. Ardvreck castle dates from the sixteenth century or perhaps slightly earlier and in Chapter 4 we told of its fate during

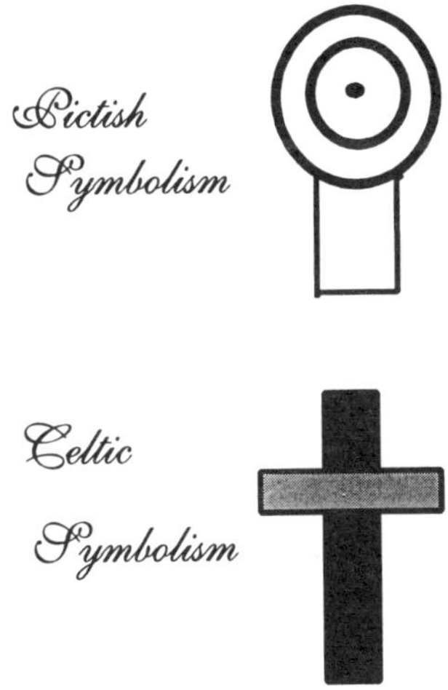

interclan rivalries between the MacLeods and the Mackenzies. The latter built Calda House (NC 243235) shortly after Ardvreck. Reports of the raiding of lands and the burning of houses by the MacKenzies in the seventeenth century imply that by that time individual buildings assigned by a clan to a clansman and his family were common. The more prosperous farmers were, by the eighteenth century, able to afford and build substantial houses though few of these are still standing..

Meantime that move to the coast had already started, some of the poorer families being attracted to fishing or by the kelp harvesting for alginate extraction. A fishing station and herring curing plant were built at Lochinver in 1775 and about that same time a fishery was also established on Tanera Mor, the largest of the Summer Isles. As we indicated in Chapter 4, these activities preceded the founding of Ullapool. In Ullapool some of the old fisheries buildings are converted to modern use, a notable example mentioned in Chapter 2, p.23, being the old red herring shed.

Crofting times

The earliest crofts now lie mostly in ruins or have been replaced by more modern buildings on the same sites. Crumbling walls of deserted crofts are often sufficiently intact to give some idea of the layout.

In some the building has clearly been on two different levels. In these, the lower level was for cattle and the higher for human occupants, the whole shared perhaps with hens roosting in the rafters.

In many of these crofts the cattle and the people entered by the same door, the cattle then moving to the lower level which ensured that their effluent did not flow back to the human quarters. On cold winter evenings the warmth generated by the animals also benefitted the humans and supplemented that from a peat fire.

Ruined crofts near the coast sometimes still show traces of outside timbered frames over which fish nets were hung to dry. Outbuildings here may have well been kilns for kelp drying, an activity, the fortunes and misfortunes of which, we described in Chapter 4.

In inland glens ruined crofts are probably symbolic of compulsory clearances which may have been transfers to coastal sites or forced emigration.

More recently abandoned crofts may be a consequence of the drift of younger members of a crofting family away from the Highlands with little remaining interest in their inheritance.

Industrial archaeology

There is not a great deal of what is fashionably termed 'industrial archaeology' in the Assynt or Coigach area. As anywhere, there are the ruins of barns or other farm buildings which have become surplus to requirements due to changes in farming practice such as a move from cattle to arable farming, or the shift from horse to tractor as beast of burden. The decline in herring fishing led to closure, or conversion to other uses of processing plants or other shore facilities. There are ruins of several mills and others have been converted to newer uses.

Prominent landmarks on our mountains, and *Suilven's World* has a generous share of these, are the Ordnance survey (OS) trig cairns, more formally called triangulation pillars (Plate IV). Modern mapping using satellite photography and other methods have made these obsolete. The OS are trying to preserve them by offering them to volunteer sponsors who will undertake to maintain them. For the hill-walker they are a friendly sight, especially when, on a misty day, they may be the only sure sign that you have scaled your target peak. To reach the top of a mountain you set out to climb still brings a glow of achievement even on a day when all you can confirm is that the inside of one cloud does look much like the inside of any other!

7 *Flora — Old and New*

Battling a tough environment

The acid, peaty soils common in *Suilven's World* are anathema to many, but clearly not to all, plants. In Chapter 5 we told how Lewisian gneiss exuded acids over millions of years as it broke down, very slowly, into sparse soils, not rich in plant nutrients. Today's peat bogs are acidic too, and although at a sweeping glance their vegetation may look a uniform golden brown, with mottled patches of darkish green, changing colour only slightly with the seasons, closer inspection reveals a more interesting picture. In a few areas near Ullapool, Elphin and Inchnadamph the base-rich soils, by contrast, give a profusion of rich grasses and more conventional British plant life. High rocky hillsides often carry only a scattering of alpine plants.

Forestry Commission plantations and most private ones are often dominated by non-native species such as Sitka spruce or lodgepole pine while remaining pockets of natural woodland often contain only one or two dominant species, most commonly birches with a few rowans or alders and, less often, isolated clusters of Caledonian pine. Quite a few of the latter are on small islets in the larger lochs where they have escaped the ravages of fire or axe and the attention of deer, sheep and other herbivores.

Visitors, at most times of year will find a variety of interesting flowers, different species catching the eye in each season. In late April or early May in deciduous woodlands primroses add a splash of delicate yellow, and at about the same time but continuing longer, come the more vivid golden yellows of gorse and broom. Bluebells follow, and a little later the paler and more delicate harebell, or 'Scottish' bluebell. At the end of June there are bogland acres of millions of fluffy white tufts of cotton grass seed heads, giving a lie to the mirage of a uniform dreariness of peat bogs (Plate VI). During the summer delicate small pink, white or purple flowered wild orchids catch the bogland walker's eye. In early autumn, especially in the woodlands, look for colourful fungi. On the hills in September the wild blaeberry, cowberry and other native shrubs are often laden with ripening fruits. The many heaths and heathers produce in late summer and autumn seas of purple, adding yet another splash of colour to the moorland, though heathers do not grow here in quite the profusion found in the drier Eastern Highlands.

In July or early August thousands of creamy white waterlilies float on beds of dark green leaves to add a splash of colour to many lochans, including some nestling in the Lewisian gneiss close to the coast roads between Achiltibuie and Drumbeg. Other well-known plants common throughout Britain also grow by the roadside and on the bogs and hills of *Suilven's World*. In all, about one third of all known species in the UK are found in the area.

The flora is full of surprises; plants such as thrift, or sea pink, grow both on sea cliffs and on the tops of mountains, but not on the ground between. When the ice cap receded, some of the first plants to colonise the area were arctic-alpine species, and indeed many such plants found here on the tops of hills grow also at sea level in the Arctic close to snowfields and glaciers. The sea pink has survived in both a coastal and a mountain environment thanks to subtle genetic differences between two strains.

Many common plants from this part of the world, as everywhere, have been used for medicinal purposes. Clansmen (and doubtless the clan chiefs as well), even perhaps the Picts in earlier days, and more recently crofters, used camomile infusions for relief of headaches and indigestion. Sloe jelly was a recommended cough remedy and a once popular healing ointment was made by pounding primrose petals in butter. The foxglove was used as a soporific and indeed its leaves and seeds are a natural source of the drug digitalis used today in purified forms for the treatment of some heart conditions. The bog-moss, *Sphagnum*, which has an important role in the formation of peat, was once used in antiseptic dressings, largely because it soaks up water and is acidic, thus resisting decay. *Lycopodium* powder, obtained from various species of club moss, was used as a surgical absorbent (as well as in the making of fireworks!). Club mosses are modern remnants of giant ancestors which formed part of the 'coal forests' that existed more than 300 million years ago. In *The Crofting Years* Francis Thompson gives an extensive list of herbal remedies used by crofters.

British national newspapers recently reported moves to enrol the bog myrtle, *Myrica gale*, as a midge repellant. This small shrub, seldom more than 40 cm tall, grows mainly in bogs. It has hitherto been of interest to botanists largely because it is one of a few non-legume species that can 'fix' nitrogen, i.e. convert atmospheric nitrogen into compounds which the plant can use for its own growth, even returning some of these compounds to the soil as a nutrient source available to other plants.

The new interest in bog myrtle stems from observations by Angus Stewart, a retired professor of pathology, that midges kept away from the plant. Exploring further, he found that an oil extracted from this sweet-scented shrub repelled midges. The professor has interested the pharmaceutical firm Efamol in plans to produce a natural insect repellant based on these oils and a pilot plant has been set up on the Isle of Skye to extract them. Experiments have shown that the oil also repels other insects, including some mosquitoes. A spokesman for Efamol was reported recently in the Financial Times to believe that 'bog myrtle could eventually be grown in plantations and cropped like tea'.

Plant distribution

Important factors that influence plant distribution include

- climate
- soil
- animal activity (including that of man)

Generally speaking, as one moves northwest through the Scottish Highlands wind strength increases and so does humidity, and the summers become cooler. All these factors lead to harsher growing conditions and these are reflected in features like lower treelines and a tendency for some species found only above, say, altitudes of 2000 feet in central Scotland, to grow down to 1000 feet in *Suilven's World.* For example, alpine heaths that are found only above 2500 feet in the Cairngorms often grow at only half that altitude in Assynt.

A few plants are tough and will grow under almost any conditions; some demand acid, others alkaline soils; some need shade, some permanent moisture, others thrive in near drought. Some succumb to being grazed, for others this is a natural form of pruning. Animals differ in grazing habits, not only in their choice of plants for food, but in how they attack those plants; deer and cattle tend to nibble, sheep and rabbits have more destructive habits, biting firmly at plants and often removing them from the soil, roots and all. Whereas grazing by appropriate animals may act as a stimulant to plant growth, over-grazing, or rough grazing, can eliminate whole species and transform the nature of a landscape. Many species have been lost to animal grazers, and a few also to human botanical 'grazers' who, all too eagerly, in the nineteenth century took specimens of rare plants for drying and preserving in their herbaria. The human threat today comes from the amateur gardener who takes specimens of rare plants that need very special conditions for survival and growth and transfers them to a suburban garden where their chances of survival are low. A more benign and generally acceptable human predator, is the photographer, who can achieve a pleasing record, in many ways surpassing that of a dried herbarium specimen, using a modern camera and colour film. However, if you want to photograph a rare, or even just an attractive even if plentiful, plant please be careful where you put your feet. Indeed, in all movements over open countryside be careful with those feet; many a delicate mountain or bogland plant cannot survive even one assault from a size 11, or even a size 7, walking boot.

It is not widely realised that when plant numbers of a species in a habitat fall below a certain critical density, survival in that habitat is already threatened because seeds are no longer produced in sufficient numbers to maintain the population. This has been a problem with some stands of Caledonian pine. At, or near this minimal survival density the result of taking or damaging just a few plants may be critical. If you do want a specimen of some plant for your garden, even if it is a variety that is plentiful and one you know will grow well there, remember it is an offence to take any plant without the permission of the owner of the land, and also that some plants are protected by law, and their uprooting (or even picking their flowers) is forbidden. Seeds of many wild species, grown under cultivation, can now be purchased from seed merchants. These are often selected strains that adapt much better than 'wild' specimens to garden environments.

If you are not familiar with Highland plants, a good place to get an introduction to local flora is the Knockan Nature trail, running in parallel with the geological trail we described in Chapter 5. Also, amateur naturalists will find a wealth of local information in Colin Scouller's booklet *An Introduction to the Flowering Plants and Ferns of Lochbroom & Assynt* prepared for the Lochbroom Field Club. A useful general guide to Highland plants is Derek Ratcliffe's *Highland Flora.* To identify individual specimens you may need a general flora; for example, W. Keble Martin's *The Concise British Flora,* or the more comprehensive *Illustrated Flora of Britain and Northern Europe* by M. Blamey and C. Grey-Wilson. There are also a number of books covering specific plant types such as ferns or fungi. Some are given in our Further Reading list.

The Knockan Cliff nature trail

The Knockan Cliff nature trail (NC 189092) is part of the Inverpolly Nature Reserve. In the main Inverpolly Reserve, not only are there several small natural birch woods, some of which also contain rowan, hazel, holly and occasionally oak and other species, but also interesting understorey plants including several ferns. In these woods and on the boglands of Inverpolly, some 350 plant species have been recorded. Experimental 'deer-proofed' plots have been set up to encourage regeneration of trees and plants under conditions where they are protected from the many red deer that roam the Reserve.

In 1992 Scottish Natural Heritage was set up as an independent Government sponsored agency charged, among other things, with the conservation and enhancement of Scotland's natural heritage. Shortly after its foundation it took over from the UK Nature Conservancy Council responsibility for many Scottish nature reserves, including Inverpolly. One of its early initiatives at Knockan was to produce revised and more informative guides to the Knockan Cliff trails.

The nature trail has a number of recommended stopping points designated by letters *A, B, C* . . . as distinct from the numbers used on the geological trail. It is worth reading the appropriate section of the trail guide obtainable for a modest sum from the Visitors centre at the Knockan Cliff car park. Not only does this explain precisely what is of interest at each point, but it gives insights into how the flora has developed since the receding of the last ice caps some 10 to 12 thousand years ago, until today.

For example, the first stopping point, *A*, is by a rock covered in whitish lichens (the lichens almost look to be part of the rock until you examine them more closely). There are literally millions of such lichen-covered rocks in *Suilven's World* (see Plates VII and VIII). The trail guide explains in detail how these primitive plants can survive on bare rock and help create small pockets of soil by trapping wind-blown particles, the remains of small insects and even bird droppings. There are many different lichens of varied colours on rocks throughout the Western Highlands. Some of them are long-established sources of dyes used in the tweed industry.

Once soil pockets are formed, if there is enough moisture, mosses may establish. Lichens do little to break down rock directly to form soil, but mosses do this by trapping moisture in the soil pockets in which they grow, thus keeping the rock wetter; in winter this moisture freezes and may crack the rock. Although this is a matter of controversy, it is possible that some mosses also release chemicals which have a weathering effect on the rock. Some larger mosses spread rapidly over wet soils, allowing seeds of bigger plants — even trees — to take root in the moist conditions and the shelter provided by the moss. At that stage dead plant material also has a role in building up the soil — forming natural mini-compost heaps.

These processes, still continuing visibly today (Plate VIII), have, as indicated, been going on since the end of the last ice age. The glaciers themselves, as they receded, left many soil pockets in the debris they had collected over several millennia. Arctic and alpine plants, then plentiful in the relatively warmer England of that time, were the first to colonise this debris. Gradually small herbs and shrubs appeared, and the lichens and then the moss carried out the process described above to create new soil and to break down even more rocks. Over hundreds of years a diverse growth pattern developed, dwarf shrubs such as crowberry and herbaceous plants on well-drained soils where there was a reasonable nutrient supply and on alkaline soils the lime-loving mountain avens became established. It is a low-growing evergreen shrub, the tough toothed leaves being deep green above, but white-felted underneath, an arctic-alpine species that is a reliable indicator of alkaline soils.

Where drainage was poor what is sometimes called a tundra-like vegetation built up with an abundance of sedges and a few dwarf willows or even birches. Unlike the situation in true Arctic tundras, which are treeless, taller woody plants gradually appeared, early-comers probably including yet taller willows and junipers. Birches soon spread to all but the most boggy tundra-like ground.

Derek Ratcliffe suggests that Caledonian pines probably reached Wester Ross about 6000 BC and gradually pushed north towards Sutherland, preceded by birch woodlands, some of which were then replaced by pines, the pine probably reaching Assynt about 3000 BC. While pine probably dominated at that stage the undergrowth in this forest would include heather, blaeberry and other plants still common today. Recent genetic studies have suggested that a type of Caledonian pine common before the ice ages might have survived these conditions in small pockets in the

Loch Maree area of Wester Ross, and that these may have been the source of the post-ice-age Highland pine forests.

Birch, juniper, hazel, ash and aspen probably continued to thrive on lime-rich soils. There were also willows in the wetter areas and rowans were widely distributed, with alder by the burns and other water channels. It is believed that at one stage on poorer soils oaks spread even further north than pines. These ancient forests supported a variety of wildlife far greater than that of today, including, as we mentioned in earlier chapters, brown bears and lynx. Today, in *Suilven's World*, with the possible exception of birch, the rowan is the commonest survivor of these ancient forest species, and there are a few rowans on the now-rather-treeless Knockan trail. Rowans are found at altitudes from sea level to 2500 ft or more. Their red berries give a blaze of colour in the autumn, at least until the birds get their fill. Several short sections of the 'wee mad road' through Inverkirkaig are bordered by rowans. What appears to be destructive bird attacks in fact explain the wide survival of the species. The seeds are protected by a hard crust impermeable to a bird's gastric juices, and therefore have a good chance of germinating wherever the bird chooses to deposit them (unless it be on the roof of your car). Apart from the rowans, all that remains at Knockan to remind us of this vast forest that probably was at its best some 4000 years ago are a few stumps.

Forest decline and after

The decline of the forest over most of the Highlands was brought about firstly by a change to a colder and wetter climate that encouraged sphagnum and other mosses under and around the tree cover. The very plants that had helped at an earlier time to build up the soil now worked to destroy the forest, for in the colder and wetter conditions dead plant material was slower to decay (indeed spaghnum also inhibits decay) and this led to the formation of peat as a soil covering. In many places this peat layer became more than a metre deep and prevented pine seedlings from taking root, and so the pine forest began to decline. Man then added to these troubles, removing, over many centuries, nearly all the older timber either by cutting or burning to clear land for grazing or to discourage predatory animals such as wolves or foxes, or by felling it for fuel or for building and also by grazing domestic animals who ate any remaining seedlings even on the less peaty ground where otherwise they may well have developed to mature trees.

The inhibitory influences of peat on plant growth may suggest that large-scale peat-cutting for fuel and for horticultural use should be encouraged. This is not so, and indeed such cutting alarms environmentalists. The reality of the situation is that one cannot turn back the clock by so simple an expedient as removing peat. Indeed, excessive cutting loses not only that vegetation that survives or thrives on peat, but usually leads to serious erosion and hydrological problems that follow removal of this water-absorbing material.

Because decay is slow in peat it also provides a natural museum for the study of plant development because most peat bands contain millions of pollen grains, each unique to a species. By identifying grains at various depths one may build up a picture of what kinds of plants were growing at specific eras in the past.

Plants that are tolerant to, and will grow in peaty acid soils include the heathers; many heathland plants produce berries which are a vital source of food for birds and small mammals such as mice. Heathers are found not only on open heathlands, but also as an undershrub in pine forests. Some, such as the early-flowering bell heather, prefer drier hillocks or slopes, whereas the cross-leaved heath prefers wetter sites. There are many related species such as the crowberry, the shoots of which, like those of heather itself, are an important foods for red grouse.

Even exposed soil in predominantly peaty areas is often acidic, cold and wet, and contains little plant nutrient. Few plants can grow in such conditions, but one or two species have adapted to such adversities, obtaining nutrients by catching and digesting insects. One of these is the butterwort, which has a single purple flower and sticky yellowish leaves. Insects caught on the leaves are trapped and slowly digested. There are several other insectivorous plants in Suilven's World, some using hairy leaves rather than natural adhesives as the trapping mechanism. Yet others, such as the bladderworts, which grow largely submerged in pools, have small bladders on their leaves which open, trap, and then digest, aquatic insects.

Ferns are another major plant group in the area. Bracken predominates, but there are many other species, including a number that grow in secluded rocky crevices often along with mosses, liverworts and lichens, their survival being possible because of a lack of competition from more robust plants coupled with protection from grazing animals.

Several centuries ago bracken was used for cattle bedding, and grazing cattle also tended to trample it, keeping it under manageable control. Now it is often burnt, either deliberately or accidentally as part of the heather burning process for regeneration of heathland for sheep grazing and grouse-raising purposes. Unfortunately, it becomes especially vigorous after burning. Although generally despised and known to be carcinogenic, bracken has one ecological point in its favour; it is a favourite breeding ground for several species of butterfly. That it is also attractive to ants who feed on a nectar produced by it is a dubious blessing, especially as the ants also feed on potential predators of this fern.

There are other classes of plant. For example, the arctic alpines that, as we have already mentioned, once grew freely in England before the Scottish glaciers receded. As Britain warmed these became extinct in the slowly warming south. Not only did the climate of the Highlands suit them, but they need open sites and cannot tolerate tree cover. Some even like acid soils, so in the UK, many now survive only in the Highlands.

The sedges are another common family, and they thrive on poorly drained peaty soils that in essence are bogs. Although, despite some of their popular names, sedges are not true grasses, one or two (e.g. deer grass) have a general appearance similar to grasses when they are not in flower. The flower stems of deer grass form dense tufts and each stem ends in a single small spikelet. The so-called cotton grasses (Plate VI) are also sedges, at least two variants being common on moorland bogs, one having single flowered spikelets and the other multiflowered spikelets. Rushes also belong to the sedge family; some members of this family prefer acidic bogs, others a base-rich bog.

Fungi

Fungi, including mushrooms and toadstools, are autumn features in Coigach and Assynt, the most striking being the white-spotted red-capped fly agaric, but the range of shapes and colours, browns, yellows, orange, grey is almost endless. The fly agaric, like many other fungi, is associated with specific plants, in its case usually the birch, although it is sometimes also found in association with pine. The link between fungi and other living plants or trees is often not a host-parasite relationship, but rather a beneficial partnership in what is called a mycorrhizal association. These 'fungus-roots' enable the plant to take up soil nutrients more effectively. Of course not all fungi are beneficial in all circumstances, as you will know all too well if you have ever had a dry-rot problem in your home. Even if a fungus is not associated with a specific host plant it is often confined to a particular environment. Although fungi are most obvious in the autumn they are present, especially under decaying logs or rotting leaves, at any time. They are more evident in autumn because that is when most of them produce their, often colourful or beautifully shaped, fruiting or spore-bearing bodies.

Many fungi have an important role in the over-all growth cycle, aiding decomposition of dead organic matter and. breaking down the cellulose and lignins found in plants into smaller components that can be used by other organisms, including bacteria, in a decay process which finally returns nutrients to the soil for recycling.

Because of their associations with certain habitats or tree or other plant species, the ideal place to look for fungi is in mixed woodland, especially if there is also a varied understorey and a range of moisture conditions.

Some people find many fungi repulsive, associating them with death and decay, perhaps even with witchcraft. However, there is a growing interest in, and appreciation of, their diversity of form and also in their potential as food. Continental Europeans have for long made greater use of fungi in cooking than we have in Britain. The naïve classification into mushrooms (edible) and toadstools (poisonous) is a gross over-simplification. But, although several species found in *Suilven's World*, including chanterelles, are edible, never, never eat fungi unless you are certain you have identified a specimen correctly, and have reliable information that it is not poisonous. There are no universal criteria for determining whether or not fungi are edible, and many edible species, including chanterelles, have near look-alikes that are poisonous. Even identification of fungi from books can be misleading unless you also have some field experience preferably obtained under tuition from a mycologist — an expert on fungi. One problem with identification from books is that colour reproduction is not always accurate, or even if it is, there may be local natural colour variations.

8 *Carnivali animali*

A first impression

First impressions are often misleading. A first experience of a single-track road may convince a driver that the only animals in the Highlands are hill sheep. These are the dominant domestic species of the twentieth century *Suilven's World,* and they emphasize their nuisance value by lying indolently on narrow strips of warm tarmac, daring one to drive around them. For a ewe and her lamb there is no better entertainment than that game of 'chicken' where each grazes contentedly on opposite verges, until you are only yards away, at which time the lamb suddenly leaps in front of your car with a plaintive bleat of 'Where's mummy?'

Then again, in certain weathers and at the right time of year, walkers, anglers, or anyone just enjoying a breath of fresh air, may think the dominant fauna is the midge, an insect with a capacity to annoy out of all proportion to its size.

Such first impressions are soon dispelled. Though not as diverse as in the heyday of the Highland forests, the present range of animal life is still more extensive than that of many parts of Britain. Some species quickly become familiar to all visitors, others are seen only by a lucky few. They vary from the domestic to the wild, with in-between, animals like feral goats and cats, descendants from once domesticated ancestors, but now living wild.

Mammals you may see range from tiny mice and voles to the mighty red deer stags, if you are lucky perhaps a 'Royal' with 14-pointer antlers — Landseer's *Monarch of the Glen* — standing over 4 feet tall at the shoulder and weighing 20 stone or more. Intermediate in size are the predatory pole cats, the pine martens and foxes, then badgers, otters and others. There are amphibians such as frogs and toads, and reptiles that include two species of lizard and the sleek adder. At the lower end of the size spectrum are a variety of insects — e.g. ants, beetles, bumble bees — and also spiders. Then there are those flying insects of which, from the human angle, the tiny midge is the least desirable.

There are birds of coast, moorland, mountain and cliff. Everybody wants to see the fabulous golden eagle, our largest bird of prey. Only the lucky, or the persistent, do.

Other favourites with visitors, even if not always with fishermen, are those amphibious mammals, the grey and the common seal. Although seals are the prime attractions of the coast, there is a wealth of other life to be seen near the shore, especially at low tide.

Some Animals to look for

Sheep apart, there are many animals to be seen or sought out. Successful sighting often depends on knowing where and when to look. We give notes on a few, omitting well-known and widely dispersed species like rabbits, mice, voles and foxes. More detailed accounts of most species, both common and rare, and their habits and habitats, are given in David Stephen's *Highland Animals* and in the Scottish Wildlife Trust's *Wildlife of Scotland.* You are more than 1000 years too late to see the last brown bear is Assynt, some 800 years too late for a reindeer and 300 years or more have passed since wolves and wild boar roamed the forests here.

Red deer. The reindeer may be gone, but today's red deer have also been in the Highlands as long as man, though it is only since the Victorian era that deer stalking has become both a sport and an industry. For many Highland estates stalking rights are a major source of income. The season for stag hunting is approximately from mid-August to mid-October. Anti-blood-sport lobbyists oppose stalking, but it is widely accepted that some culling of deer is needed to keep numbers in check and to maintain reasonable natural balances, and that modern controlled hunting by adequately trained marksmen is a humane method of achieving that end. Most estates take positive steps to ensure that stalkers can shoot to kill cleanly before allowing them to take part in a cull. A culling rate of something like one sixth of the stag numbers each year is generally regarded as necessary to maintain a stable and healthy population.

We have referred to the adverse effect of deer grazing on regeneration of trees. Evidence of the devastation from grazing is clear in the Inverpolly Nature Reserve, where some plots close to the Achiltibuie Road are enclosed by deer fences. Even a casual comparison between the flora in these plots and that on adjacent unfenced ground highlights the effects of deer, and of course, other grazing animals such as sheep, on vegetation.

It is hard to apportion damage between different grazers, but there is ample evidence that even where sheep are excluded and deer alone have access the damage to young trees and certain other plants is appreciable. The amount of damage depends both on population density, and on what alternative, or preferred foods, are available.

Although red deer are about as plentiful as sheep, spotting them at the height of summer in the middle of the day may call for an excursion away from roads and into the hills, as well as a sharp eye. The alternative is an early morning or late evening drive to a spot where deer are known to congregate or to come down from the hills to a loch or burn to quench their thirst.

In the hills, even if you see no deer you are almost certain to spot their droppings and in bogland to see distinctive hoof prints as evidence of their presence. With such tell-tale signs, you may wonder where, especially in open moorland, they hide. They are often well camouflaged and remain still for long periods and even if you do not see them, the odds are they have spotted you, for deer are more adept at observing us than we are at spotting them.

Red deer are the largest land animals in *Suilven's World.* Their size and weight depend to some extent on habitat and more particular on availability of food. We have hinted at 20 stone stags, but weights of 14 to 16 stone are more common, and hinds are often only about half that weight. Each sex live in separate herds for most of the year, the stags invading hind territory in the rutting season in September and October, when the males may be heard bellowing as they gather their harems. A stag's reign as monarch of a harem is often brief and a matter of dispute with other stags. Modern research has exploded the oft-quoted Gaelic myth that

Thrice the age of a horse is the age of a man
Thrice the age of a man is the age of a stag.

It is only during the last 60 years that serious studies have been made of deer ecology and of methods to control the population. The Deer (Scotland) Bill of 1959, among other things, set up a Red Deer Commission. The Commission's first report described its creation as 'the first comprehensive attempt to deal with a controversial problem which has vexed the Highlands for the best part of two centuries.' It is impossible to please everybody when dealing with controversial issues, especially if birds or animals are involved, but the work of the Red Deer Commission has met with wide approval.

Roe deer. The smaller roe deer have a different lifestyle and the problems they create are not identical to those attributed to red deer. Because they move largely in forests or in open woodland where they can find both shade in summer and cover in winter and enjoy the leaves, buds, fruit and twigs of many species it is not surprising that they destroy a great deal of flora, including seedlings and young trees. Protection against them is essential in young plantations.

Whereas red deer are often seen in herds, the smaller roe deer usually move singly or in pairs. Their summer coat is sometimes described as 'foxy' red while the winter coat is grey, often with a tinge of brown.

The mountain hare. Unlike its better-known cousin, the brown hare, the mountain hare has, like the stoat, a winter coat of white. They frequent the slopes and ridges of often fairly barren hills and mountains, and are happy to dwell above the winter snowline, making, if necessary, daily excursions to lower levels to feed on heather shoots or frosted sedges such as cotton grass, but quickly returning to snow-covered ground, where that white coat is a useful camouflage. Although they sometimes feed in large groups in severe weather, they are usually seen singly, or in sets of two or three. They are basically wanderers, often moving from one side of a hill to the other seeking food or protection from wind and blizzards. They shelter in natural holes or sometimes burrow in peat.

In the spring moult winter coats give way to dark brown fur with a hint of blue; whence the alternative popular name *blue hare*. They are slower movers than the common hare and frequently, when you come upon one, it will run only a short distance, then turn to give you a quizzical 'what do you think you're doing here?' look. Though they sometimes come lower, you are most likely to find the species above the 1500 ft contour, but not on every hill.

The pine marten. This sleek climber is sometimes referred to as 'the weasel of the trees', or as the sweet marten (to distinguish it from the foul marten, or polecat). Pine martens were once widely distributed in Britain, living mainly in forests. They decreased in numbers with the cutting of the trees, and many were caught in gin traps when those monstrosities were still legal. In the Western Highlands in the early 1900s only a few martens remained, but they are now on the increase in *Suilven's World* and other parts of Wester Ross, having adapted their lifestyle to survive in dry rocky regions, though still not averse to a frolic in the pines. Martens feed largely on small rodents such as voles and on small birds, though they are occasional raiders of poultry runs and also prey on game birds, thus ensuring they are not universally popular. Sightings are possibe at all times of day, but martens usually feeds in the evening, night or early morning. Near sunset, or shortly after sunrise are likely times to spot them. They have a cream or yellow to orange throat patch, a somewhat variable distinguishing feature, and are about the body size of, though rather longer than, a domestic cat, growing to some 2 ft 6 in. overall length, some ten inches of that being a bushy tail.

Polecats. Are polecats in *Suilven's World* true polecats or feral 'polecat ferrets'? Whether they are the real thing or feral descendants of escaped ferrets, these animals have a dubious reputation as a result of their somewhat catholic appetites, eating game birds, eggs of many species, voles, mice and rats, adders, frogs and fish.

Unlike the pine marten, the polecat is not a good tree climber, but is both a fast ground-mover and a good swimmer. They mark their terriory with a malodorous secretion from a stink gland, and it is this that earns that 'foul marten' tag.

Wildcats. These allegedly savage felines are sometimes said to be untameable, though many experts assert they may be tamed if caught young enough. A night hunter, at home in deep forests or on the mountains, the true Scottish wildcat, if indeed it still exists, is seldom seen and is certainly less common than the feral 'domestic cat gone wild'. Doubt about survival of true wildcats arises because it and the feral counterpart have interbred to an extent where some scientists argue there is no such thing as a 'pure' wildcat, although the latter pre-dated the domestic cat in Britain by some 8000 years. Until recently, the accepted distinguishing feature of a true wildcat was a tail less tapered than that of descendants from domestic cats, and ringed in black. Genetic evidence has thrown doubt on the value of this marker, first described by the Museum of Natural History in 1907 as a definitive characteristic of the Scottish wildcat.

Wild goats. Scottish wild goats are descendants of domestic goats that have long become feral. They are more common on or near An Teallach (NH 064842) than in Coigach or Assynt. They may descend to low levels in winter or even early spring if the snow is slow to thaw, but are more often seen on the hills. Domestic goats that become feral revert after a few generations to the Persian wild goat type. Colour varies, but most are predominantly black with brown, grey, cream or even white markings. They often move in small groups or herds and usually tolerate humans providing they do not come too close. If you are downwind of a feral billy goat you may well smell him before you see him, or before he sees you.

Badgers. Badgers are squat large-framed, some think almost bear-like, animals with characteristic white faces. Like the pine marten, polecat and otter, badgers are members of the weasel family They are less common in *Suilven's World* than in parts of lowland Scotland. They avoid marshes or boggy ground and like dry hillocky areas. Formidable and tough if needs be, they do not spoil for a fight, attacking man or other animals only as a last resort. However, a dog that attacks or threatens a badger risks being badly mauled. Their sets are identifiable by obvious excavations where they remove large quantities of soil to make the extensive burrows in which they take a bedding of hay and bracken. Foxes often make a home in unoccupied badgers sets and dirty surroundings indicate this has happened, for the badger is a tidy house-keeper. We understand badgers may even tolerate a fox as a tenant providing the fox keeps to parts of the set not in use by the badgers themselves.

You are unlikely to see badgers in the daytime, except perhaps during the spring mating season. They feed mainly on small animals such as rodents, slugs, earthworms and caterpillars, also on some wild fruits and grasses. They take a delight in destroying wasps nests and eating the young grubs.

Otters. Normally, an otter swims with only its rather flat head above the water, although it may pause and raise its head above the surface much as a seal does. They may be seen on the sea, in rivers and burns, or as they wander across the land. David Stephen, in *Highland Animals,* reports sightings on hill contours over 1000 ft, although it is primarily a water animal. Although they have this reputation as wanderers, there are also indications that they observe some territorial rights. Despite being at times a land hunter, the otters' diet is mainly fish, eels being a favourite, but they are (like us) not averse to the occasional salmon. If you see a half-eaten salmon on the bank of the Kirkaig an otter is the likely culprit.

Despite a superficial resemblance to seals, otters are web-footed weasels, well adapted to a land and water existence. Your best chance of spotting one is in quiet coastal bays or rivers, and although they are largely nocturnal we have seen them in the middle of the day.

Adders. The adder is the only true snake found in the Highlands — the slow-worm is not a snake, but a legless lizard. Notices that say *Beware of adders* do not always mean that there are adders about. Some land-owners find these warnings more effective than a 'Keep out' sign. Most of us have little to fear from adders, even if they are present, for, although poisonous, they are shy, and are more likely to be attacked by people who have an unreasoned fear of them and who may beat or stone one to death. Unless you have an unusually violent reaction to the venom, although adder bites are likely to produce more pain than a wasp sting, together with some sickness, perhaps temporary paralysis in the neighbourhood of the bite and a

headache, they hardly ever prove fatal. Moreover, you are unlikely to be bitten unless you tread on, or play with, one.

Do not believe anyone who tells you they saw an adder at least six — or even three — feet long. They seldom exceed two feet in length. They can be distinguished from slow-worms by their markings, especially a dark zig-zag along the spine, the male having a more contrasting pattern than the female. From time to time they shed their skin completely and after doing so the new skin pattern can be eye-catching. They sun themselves on rocks on a warm day, but will usually move away as you approach, except perhaps in the spring when they tend to be lethargic after their winter hibernation.

As we have already mentioned, many animals common to the rest of the UK will be seen in *Suilven's World*. These include rabbits, brown hares, hedgehogs, foxes, moles, shrews. various voles, bats, stoats and weasels, mice, rats, lizards, frogs, toads and numerous flies and insects, red and (unfortunately) grey squirrels, (and even more unfortunately) the imported mink.

Birds

The golden eagle. Every visitor to *Suilven's World* wants to see a golden eagle. Keep a sharp lookout and you will improve your chances of seeing these fine birds of prey if you choose your exploration area carefully — and that may involve a longish walk. As we explained in Chapter 2, that large bird atop a roadside telephone or electricity pole is almost certainly a buzzard, not an eagle. The future of the now-protected golden eagle looked bleak at the height of the Highland sheep boom, the bird being no favourite of the sheep farmer. It was less of a problem in the deer forests and had a better chance of survival, despite, even there, being hunted by farmers and collectors for its skin and its eggs.

It has increased in numbers during the present century. Eagles lay claim to large territories, and it has been suggested that one pair may be the entire species population over as much as 16 000 acres. Although any pair needs a large hunting ground for survival, there may be some overlap of areas used by different pairs. They feed on a range of victims including the mountain hare (no wonder it needs that camouflaging coat of white in winter), rabbits, and carrion (mostly of red deer or sheep), grouse, ptarmigan as well as a number of sea birds and young deer or lambs (though again usually as carrion despite the bird's once-bad reputation among shepherds).

We have on several occasions spotted eagles soaring above Loch Tuart (NC 103055) between Sgurr an Fidhleir (NC 095055) and Beinn an Eoin (NC 105064). Both these peaks are possible vantage points for spotters. We hasten to add, however, that on not all of our trips to these hills have we made a sighting. Generally speaking they are most likely to be seen where there are cliffs that will provide safe nesting sites.

Buzzards. The best known among other sizeable birds of prey is the buzzard. These you may well see atop that telephone or electricity pole perhaps on an autumn, or even a winter, day. Buzzards are usually a little less than two feet in length from head to tail, while golden eagles are up to half as long again.

Red grouse. The most famous moorland game bird is the red grouse, common in suitable habitats throughout Scotland and Northern England, but other moorland birds include moorhens and various plover. During the 1990s there has been concern about a decline in the grouse population. The well-being of the species depends partly on land management practices such as choosing the appropriate time of year for, and the right amount of, heather burning to encourage the growth of young shoots on which the grouse feed. Some claim that in recent years bad burning practices may have triggered a population decline. If so, this may be a consequence of using smaller or less experienced labour forces to control burning.

Ptarmigan. This is our favourite mountain bird. You are not likely to see these below 1500 feet, and more likely at 2000 feet or more above sea level. Their winter white is a suitable camouflage in the snow and it is replaced by a greyish brown summer plumage that makes them far from easy to spot on a rocky mountain top. They are often seen where there are shrub heaths, for the shoots of heather, crowberry and blaeberry form their main diet. In the spring they nest in a bed of moss, often in the shelter of a rock, the hatch consisting of some half dozen chicks and these are, like the parents, but with rather different patterns, well camouflaged to blend in with lichen covered rocks. The chicks are active and fast movers. On Quinag one year we had to literally watch our step to avoid planting a heavy boot on a darting youngster, the mother taking little apparent responsibility for her off-springs' somewhat erratic wanderings on a well-used path not far from a cliff-edge.

Just as many of the animals found in *Suilven's World* are common throughout Britain, so too are many of the birds, both permanent settlers and migratory. Some, like the cuckoo, arrive a little later each year than they do further south. In forests and moorland black crows are common, and in timbered country there is a smaller population of woodpeckers. One evening some years ago we spotted, or we should say we first heard, one of the latter beating a tattoo on a hydro-electric pole between Achiltibuie and Culnacraig. The species became extinct in the Highlands some 150 years ago, but during this century they have returned to breed again and are now on the increase.

Several kinds of sea birds are probably more common here than almost anywhere else in the UK. In winter, the region, together with many other parts of Scotland, plays host to birds that depart each spring for more northern breeding grounds — Iceland, Greenland or Scandinavia. These winter visitors include the goldeneye duck and barnacle and other geese. Throughout the year the coast is frequented not only by the common herring gull, but shags and cormorants are to be seen diving for fish off-shore, while the cliffs provide nesting grounds for fulmars and Arctic and common terns, gannets, guillemots and kittiwakes. The cliffs around Rubha Coigeach (NB 981181) and the Point of Stoer (NC 021356) are excellent places for sea-bird watchers. Further north Handa Island (NC 135480), is a famed bird sanctuary. There is a resident RSBP warden and visitors must follow clear defined tracks. Allow a day to visit the Island, including the drive to, and boat trip from, Tarbert (NC 163488). At Stoer or at Handa you are likely to see, and perhaps be 'dive-bombed' by a great skua or an Arctic skua, the bullies of the sea-bird world, both attacking in flight smaller sea-birds such as gulls or terns when carrying food, forcing them to drop it so that the skuas can retrieve it.

Eider ducks swim close to the shore and oystercatchers frequent sandy beaches such as those at Achnahaird (NC 019138) (Plate II) or Achmelvich (NC 054249). Herons, dippers and several species of divers are among the many birds found near rivers and burns.

The shoreline

Land, or amphibious, animals are only a small portion of Highland animal life. An oft neglected area for fauna is the meeting point between land and sea, the coastal strip between low and high water marks. At low tide an exploration of shoreline and rock pools can be fascinating.

A range of crabs and smaller creeper-crawlies lurk beneath the rocks. Blue mussels, winkles, white barnacles cling among sea anemones to stones. Small fish and minute crustaceans swim in rock pools and off-shore at the warmer times of year there are often Portuguese men-of-war.

Sit near the shore, and an inquisitive seal may take a peep at you, or you may spot them basking on wave-lapped rocky ledges, perhaps even see a dolphin frolicking at sea, as well as cormorants diving for fish or just looking doleful on an isolated ledge or rock.

For many visitors a highlight is that spotting of a seal, or better, a group of seals basking on rocks. There are two seal types — the grey and the common — off the shore of *Suilven's World*. You may well spot one, or both, on a coastal walk. On boat trips from Ullapool, Achiltibuie, Lochinver or Kylesku, a highlight is often a close approach to some rocky ledge where seals bask.

Seals lazing on rocks, slithering effortless into and out of the water, uttering the occasional bark, have won them a place in human affections. Fishermen, however, see them in a different light from the landlubber. The seal's prolific breeding rate and seemingly insatiable appetite for fish makes them view the species as a threat to fish stocks. A recent report on a six year study carried out by Aberdeen University suggests that while common seals eat herring and sprat in winter and sand eels and octopus in summer, there is little evidence that they are, as is often claimed, depleting salmon stocks. Many fishermen disagree, and there is some evidence that seals may poach salmon from, and may also damage, nets. There are also claims from fishermen that seals may open lobster creels and steal catches. Whatever the facts and the economic implications, seal culls are a long established way of keeping the population under control. Some culling methods are of questionable morality, and conservationists have not been slow to criticise. Public sympathy for apparently innocuous seals basking on rocks and sandbanks, play into the hands of those opposed to culls. Major scientific issues about natural balance are involved and we shall not dilute your pleasure of watching seals in your leisure moments by urging you to take sides in the controversy over culling. Opposition is directed especially to culling of grey seals. Common seals are often killed individually by fishermen in the sea and the practice attracts less attention, and so indirectly less criticism.

Grey seals. Grey and common seal differ both in appearance and in breeding habits. Grey seals mate, and the cows give birth to their pups, on shore. Reputedly the largest wild animal to be seen on British shores, the seal bulls are some three times the weight of a Highland stag. The grey seals, again unlike the common seal, form colonies and groups in designated spots for breeding, returning it seems, to the same sites each year. After weaning their pups the cows mate and return to the sea where they will often be spotted in coastal waters during the summer, before they move out to sea and then return to the breeding grounds in twos and threes during the autumn.

The world population of grey seals is relatively small. A large proportion of that population is in Scottish waters. Their need to come ashore to breed makes them especially vulnerable. Arguments against culling — or at any rate for strict control of culling — are stronger for this species than they might be for the common seal.

Common seals. Unlike the grey seal, the common seal does not come ashore to mate or give birth. The pups, unlike those of the grey seal, are active and able to swim from birth. The adults may be distinguished from the grey seal by their snub noses and slanting nostrils, although they are also grey in colour. They enjoy playing in the water and may often be seen frolicking off, or close to, the shore.

Butterflies, moths and other insects.

Between that obnoxious flier the midge and the wide range of birds there are several butterflies and many moths, as well as bumble bees, bats and beetles. The Azure Hawker, a brilliant blue and black dragonfly almost unique to the Western Highlands, is common near woodlands. Caterpillars are found on heathland and peat bogs including the bright green one of the Emperor moth. You are less likely to see the moth itself, as it flies largely at night. Eggars, brown moths that fly by day, are superabundant in late summer; their caterpillars are large, brown and hairy and are common in the heather.

The mighty midge(t)

The midge has a reputation out of proportion to its size and its life span of only a few hours. What midges lack in size and life span, they make up for by sheer numbers. But first the good news; only the females of six out of more than 100 species found in Britain bite, and midges do not like bright light or strong winds. So if you go out only on bright or windy days you should have few problems. But *Suilven's World* does have that dull or still day when you are wise to fraternise only with male midges or females of a non-biting species. The bad news is that if a midge lands on your skin with intent it is almost certainly one of the six biting species that is giving you her attention and she will take her mission seriously, for she has a pressing need for a feed of blood before laying her eggs. After you are bitten, it is little consolation to know that deer or sheep blood would have done just as well, and that those animals find midges as irritating as we do.

Some repellants are more effective than others and not everyone finds midge bites seriously irritating. If you suffer intense irritation, antihistamine creams usually provide relief.

9 *Fish and fishing*

An angler's paradise

We are not fisherpersons (our publisher insists on politically correct language no matter how silly it sounds), but that does not mean we have no interest in fish or in fishing for pleasure or for profit. We admire the patience of anglers and their evident skill as they sit for hours in boats or on a river bank, casting a fly or, when fortune favours them, playing a fish.

We respect also the skills of those who make their living by fishing at sea and we know the risks they take. We realise too that game fishing or sea-angling for pleasure is a challenging sport. *Suilven's World* has a long association with sea fishing, an occupation we consider later, but from the visitors' viewpoint, and also for many residents, the attractions for anglers are the rivers, burns and lochs.

The Coigach Lochs, Lurgainn (NC 110090), Bad a' Ghaill (NC 075105), Osgaig (NC 044120), Sionascaig (NC 120140) and those of Assynt including Loch Assynt (NC 210245), also Cam Loch (NC 210135), Veyatie (NC 180135) and Fionn Loch (NC 130175) on the Ross-Sutherland border and dozens of other lochs and lochans are among Scotland's better known trout fisheries. Rivers such as the Kirkaig (NC 100183), the Inver (NC 120236) and the short turbulent Garvie (NC 040133) attract hundreds of fishermen each year. Wild brown trout provide excellent sport in all these, and where there is appropriate access to the sea, as in the case of Lochs Osgaig and Assynt, for example, sea trout and salmon are further targets for the angler. Angling makes an important contribution to the Highland economy.

The catch

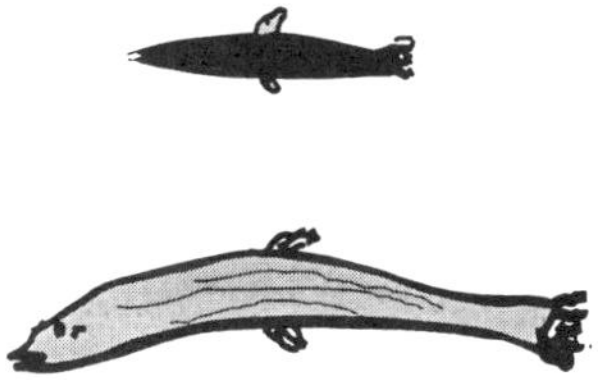

The one that got away

Every angler dreams of catching a large fish (never quite as large as the one that got away), but there is nearly always a trade-off between availability and size. Some lochs give good prospects of a large bag of small fish, each weighing less than a pound, while others hold out (usually slight) hopes of landing that 12 pounder. Loch Borrolan (NC 265108) and Loch Urigill (NC 245110) both have reputations for good bags of free-rising trout; especially during the mayfly hatch in late June. Although relatively small in size, these fish are great fighters. Growth rates of brown trout are determined largely by temperature and acidity of lochs. Low temperatures and high acidity both reduce the rate.

A few deep lochs such as Assynt and Cam Lochs contain ferox or cannibal trout. These monsters are not a separate species, but trout that first develop a taste for smaller trout and then move to deeper waters where they feed on char or other fish and eventually end up weighing 20 lb. or more. They can generally only be caught by trolling, or spinning a large bait at depth. Modern biological evidence suggests that a genetic factor may explain the ferox's inclination for a fish diet, and it is thought that the strain may bave evolved shortly after the end of the last ice age. This argument is supported by the fact that ferox trout are largely confined to deep glacially-formed lochs.

Fionn Loch is the source of the Kirkaig river, a stream beloved by salmon fishermen. The Kirkaig falls are, however, an upper barrier for these, so it is for trout that the Loch is famed.

Fishermen, knee-deep in their waders, are a common sight near the outflow to the river, and the loch is also fished from boats.

Walk from the Inverkirkaig carpark to the falls and loch and you pass a number of fishing beats. Especially from July to the end of the season, you may spot determined anglers hoping to land a salmon from one of the deep pools as far upstream as the foot of the Kirkaig Falls (NC 111179). The Kirkaig is a fast flowing river with a gravel or rocky base that ensures cool clear waters with good oxygenation — ideal for salmon and sea trout. The Viking invaders were clearly impressed by Scottish salmon, their name, *lax,* for salmon, persisting to this day in the Laxford river and Laxford Loch (NC 200495) north of Scourie. Salmon or trout fishing from boats is popular on lochs like Osgaig and Assynt, and on these and smaller lochs you may see boats tied up when they are not being put to use by determined anglers.

Most fishing waters are private and permits are required either from a landowner, from an hotel that has fishing rights (and some only make fishing available to guests) or from a local angling club.

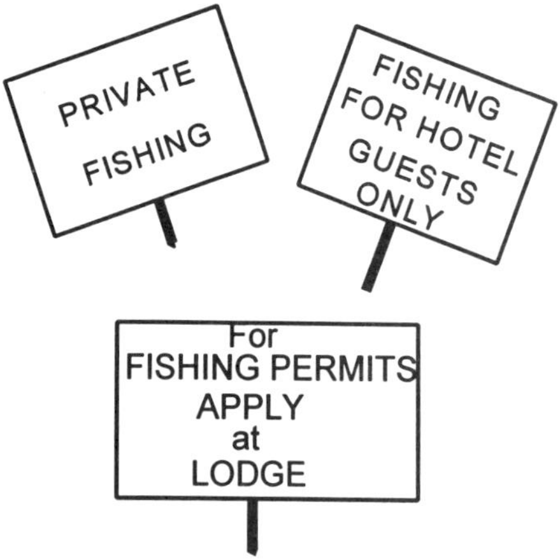

Major hotels in *Suilven's World* and other parts of Wester Ross and Sutherland usually have rights for trout, and often also for salmon fishing, on lochs, burns or rivers that they make available, often at a charge, to guests. Some operate rotas or draw lots each day to apportion the beats in a way that does not favour some anglers at the expense of others. Fishing is available on many smaller lochs in North Assynt by arrangement with the Assynt Angling Club or the North Assynt Estate.

Gillies are often available and it may be possible to arrange locally for beginners to receive tuition. Appropriate equipment is essential. Shops that sell angling gear are usually happy to help, but an angling friend is probably the best source of advice about minimum requirements. The proprietors of hotels that cater for the angler usually know the best conditions and seasons to fish the various waters and the most appropriate tackle and lures, such as the right flies. Hotel chefs are often happy to cook your catch for breakfast, or to store fish for a few days in their freezer if you want to take your prizes back home.

The season starts in March, running to September for trout and October for salmon. Sunday is the salmon's statutory day of rest from predatory anglers. The season for salmon is best from July onward, while late June, July and September are usually regarded as good months for trout, but there are local variations, some lochs being especially good only for a few peak weeks.

Be alert to the safety of others while fishing. Hooking a member of your party, or some other party, is not a fair catch. Whether angling on loch, river, or at sea sensible precautions when casting are essential. Some nasty accidents have occurred by a cast fouling power lines near rivers or lochs. Remember too, it is a punishable offence to discard broken lines, hooks, or sinkers. There is a real danger that birds may swallow these with fatal consequences, or that animals (included humans) may be injured by a barbed hook.

Sea angling

Ullapool, Lochinver, and to a lesser extent Achiltibuie and Kylesku are commercial fishing bases. Sea-angling cruises can often be arranged from these centres and are aimed both at the serious sportsman and those who want to fish for pleasurable adventure or just for fun. Most cruises operate close to the shore and the skippers will usually provide basic tackle and bait or tell you where you may get these. Cod, ling and haddock are often caught and more experienced anglers sometimes hook skate, halibut and even the occasional shark. Be properly clothed and equipped for sea-angling and be alert to the safety of others. As for freshwater angling, hooking a member of your party, or some other party, is a foul and a line entangled with a boat's propeller may cause inconvenience and even threaten safety.

Commercial fishing

If you come to *Suilven's World* to sample local food, fish will play as prominent, or even a more prominent role, than game. Lochinver is primarily a white fish port with good landings of haddock and cod, but lobster, scallops, mussels and prawns are all landed in substantial numbers in the relevant seasons, many for export to England and other EC countries. Samples find their way to local hotels and restaurants many of whom have arrangements with a local fisherman to ensure delivery of choice specimens within hours of catching. Some hoteliers even set their own lobster pots, or collect mussels when the tide is right.

Coastal middens of fish shells dating back several thousand years reflect the long history of fishing in Wester Ross and Sutherland, and the later bestowal of names like Laxford indicates Viking appreciation of our fish.

The most obvious new development in commercial fishing is fish farming. Salmon farming is an activity made all too visible by moored cages in sheltered lochs and bays. Farming is now spreading to shellfish, including oysters and scallops and even to more exotic white fish such as halibut.

There are several salmon and trout hatcheries producing young fish both to supply farms and for stocking lochs and rivers. Artificial stocking of rivers with salmon has not proved entirely satisfactory, for whereas native salmon return to the same river each year, those released from hatcheries where the ova may come from various sources, often lack the inborn ability, probably part of the fish's genetic make-up, to make return journeys from sea to the appropriate river for breeding purposes. In *Suilven's World* some lochs have been stocked with sea trout, but there is little anecdotal evidence about, let alone scientific assessment of, its success.

Fish farming in general is a development that has caused controversy. Concentrated feeding and use of chemicals to control diseases that spread rapidly in crowded conditions in fish cages moored in sea lochs, cause pollution problems that must be faced.

Many people consider the quality and flavour of a farmed salmon does not equal that of its wild counterpart. There are differences in flesh texture that enable the expert to distinguish farmed from wild salmon, but as in all animal products, there are wide variations between individuals, these probably being more marked among wild specimens as a result of environmental differences as well as genetic ones. It is probably fair to say that nothing can beat the flavour of a good wild salmon, but that the farm product tends to be more uniform, though perhaps a little blander, than the best wild salmon.

With shellfish there do not appear to be serious pollution problems, and the farmed mussel is often cleaner and less gritty than some natural ones. Oyster farming has been developed successfully near Drumbeg using Pacific oysters which have the commercial advantage that they do not breed in cool Scottish waters. Their need of warmer seas for breeding means that those from Scottish waters may be eaten throughout the year without first checking whether or not there is a letter *r* in the month. We find the farmed product very edible, although we are not connoisseurs of the oyster.

We have little doubt though, that you will have to look far to beat Scotland's west-coast wild prawns, scallops or lobsters. We hope we are wrong in our suspicion that over-fishing problems may be depleting stocks.

The traditional wild white fish of the region was once the herring. Even before there was a local industry, the Dutch visited Loch Broom in sailing boats to exploit the then almost unlimited supplies. Indeed, these visitors probably provided the inspiration for the local industry we mentioned in chapters 2 and 4, first with the curing stations on Tanera Mor and Isle Martin, then at Ullapool. Overfishing left stocks in Loch Broom depleted as early as 1820 and they were virtually wiped out by 1880. Modern trawler fishing methods using drift nets have led to all-too-well-known depletion in recent years even of deep sea stocks not only of herring, but also of many other species.

The largest commercial catches in recent years from Ullapool have been from shoals of mackerel that appear off the coast in late summer and autumn, and as we mentioned in Chapter 2, these are sold to the klondikers from eastern Europe.

For the local fisherman in his small boat, or the crofter or visitor casting a line from a coastal rock, there are still possible catches of cod, whiting, haddock and hake, but by all accounts these too are suffering the problems of over-fishing, a problem that has accelerated in the last quarter century as increasing numbers of former North Sea fishermen have turned their attention to West-coast fishing beds. Fishermen based at Ullapool or Lochinver have to venture into ever deeper waters for supplies of cod and haddock.

Appendix A

Grid References

What is more irritating than learning about a place of interest, but being unable to find it? Told that *The Knockan Cliffs lie some 12 miles north of Ullapool,* you have only a vague idea where they are and may take a long time to find them on a map because (a) they are not *exactly* north of Ullapool, and (b) you do not know that they are close to the left-hand side of the A835 as you travel north. These more precise indicators, make it is easier to find the cliffs, but instructions become verbose, even tedious.

If you have an accident in the hills and have to leave an injured person to seek help, it may cost a life if you can only tell a mountain rescue team that you left the victim *in a steep gully on the west face of the hill about half a mile, you think, from the summit.* Giving a precise location could save hours, perhaps make the difference between finding the victim weak but alive before nightfall, or as a frozen corpse after first light next day. Precise locations on a map are specified by a *grid reference*. This pinpoints a location to within about 100 metres on an Ordnance Survey 1:50 000 *Landranger* map. All emergency and rescue services use the system.

Instructions for giving a reference are included in recent editions of the Landranger series. On these maps 2 cm corresponds to 1km or 1¼ in. corresponds approximately to 1 mile. We describe the method here using a specific example to specify a point that is easily identified directly, namely the junction of the coast road from Lochinver to Kylesku via Drumbeg, the B869, with the main road north, the A894. The point is about 2 miles south of Kylesku, and given that information, including the road numbers, it is easy to find the junction on the Landranger map, *Sheet 15, Loch Assynt and surrounding area,* so in practice you hardly need a grid reference, but it is a good example to demonstrate the method.

References are based on the (British) National Grid. The country is divided first into large squares each identified by a two-letter combination. Each such square corresponds to a land area of 100 000 square kilometres, i.e. each side represents a land distance of 100 kilometres, or on these maps with scale 2cm = 1km, a a large map square has each side 2 metres. Since the area of any one map in the series is only 80×80 sq.cm, i.e. each side of the map area is only 80 cm, each larger grid square spans more than one sheet, and often one sheet covers parts of more than one square. The two-letter designations appear at each corner of the map sheet and adjacent to any boundary points where the designation changes. On sheet 15, NB is the designated square at the top and bottom left margins and NC the designated square at the top and bottom right margins. The boundary between NB and NC is marked near the top and bottom margins of the map, 8 cm from the left margin.

This general layout is indicated in the diagram, where the square represents the complete map area.

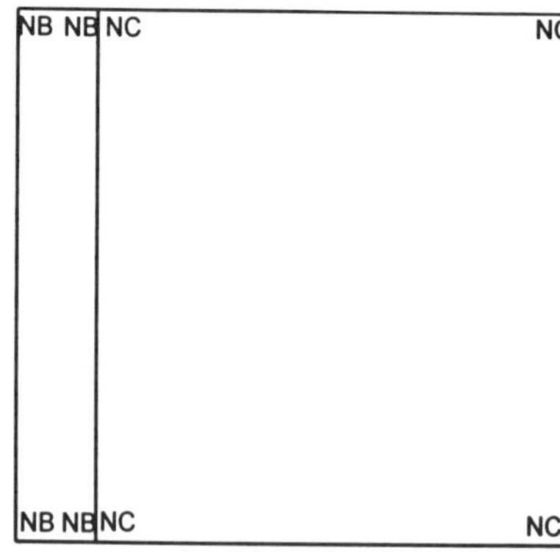

On the map the road junction for which we want a grid reference is clearly in the NC square, so we use NC as the first part of our reference. The map is divided into smaller squares by blue lines 2cm apart (corresponding to a distance of 1 km) and running south to north and west to east. At the top and bottom margins (again in blue) are successive two figure numbers at the end of each line. From left to right on the south to north lines on sheet 15 these numbers are 96, 97, 98, 99 for square NB. The next line, marking the boundary between NB and NC, is numbered 00 and the following lines 01, 02, 03, 04, . . ., 35, 36. For technical reasons the corner numbers have a small and raised ooo appended, but ignore this for a grid reference. These two-digit numbers are repeated on each line at intervals from top to bottom of the map.

Similarly starting at the bottom left of the map and moving upward each blue line has an increasing two figure designation 00, 01, 02, . . ; 39, 40. These numbers, too, are repeated on each line at intervals across the map to the right margin.

We use these numbers to complete our grid reference. We first assign three digits, called the *eastings,* to part-determine a point. The first two digits are the number allocated to the vertical grid line *immediately to the left of the required point*. For our road junction, inspecting the map shows this is 23. Now we estimate the distance of the junction, on a scale of 10 units, between the vertical lines labelled 23 and 24. This is clearly not quite one quarter of the distance between the lines, so we assign a number 2. Combining these with the 23 we get *232*, a three-digit number called the *eastings* for our point. We now assign a further three digits called the *northings*. The first two are the digits of the number on the horizontal line *immediately below the required point*. For our road junction this is 31. We now estimate the distance of the junction on a scale of 10 units, between the horizontal lines labelled 31 and 32. It is clearly a little more than one third of the way, so 4 is a reasonable estimate. Our *northing* for the point is thus *314*. The final grid reference is obtained by placing first the *easting* and then the *northing* after the grid letters, giving in this example NC 232314.

Use the same method for any other clearly defined point. To check that you have mastered the system what is the point with grid reference NC 251216? The answer is given near the foot of this page.

For a general area such as a loch, town or mountain ridge there is no unique reference, but we can easily give some reference that clearly indicates the feature. Choose a point near the feature centre unless there is some specific part of it that you want to indicate, such as the highest point on a ridge, or the northern extremity of a loch. For Loch Assynt, an appropriate though not unique, reference would be NC 205250, giving a point near the middle of that loch. A unique reference for the eastern extremity of Loch Assynt is NC 248221. A grid reference specifies a point to within approximately 100 metres, even if you are not certain whether the third digit of an easting or a northing should be, say, *2* or *3*.

For mountains it is usual to specify the highest point, which is often shown by a spot height or an Ordnance Survey triangulation pillar (a blue triangle with a central dot on the map). That on Cul Mor (Plate IV) has a grid reference NC 162119.

If it is clear that all *eastings* and *northings* refer to a specific lettered square, e.g. NC, we may omit the letters, but for clarity in this book we have always give these, because some of our references are to other lettered squares on other sheets. For example, the reference for Dundonnell hotel, on sheet 19, is NH 065893.

The answer to the query above is that NC 251216 specifies Inchnadamph hotel.

We have ended this appendix with two examples involving hotels. A psychologist would probably claim that tells you something significant about us.

Appendix B

Gaelic and Viking names

Gaelic place names dominate *Suilven's World*, with a sprinkling of Viking ones. *Suilven* is particularly interesting; it is believed to be a hybrid of the Viking, or Norse, *Suil* (pillar) and a corruption *ven* of the Gaelic *Beinn*. Variations in spelling of Scottish place or feature names are common and they often differ between books or maps. This reflects divergences between written and spoken Gaelic and also the intervention of external influences such as anglicization of some words (e.g. *Ben* for *Beinn*).

Pronunciation is a problem for non-Gaelic speakers. It is impossible to give complete rules without delving into long lists of exceptions or special cases and also because there are variations from district to district. A few guide books give a phonetic indication of pronunciation that will be understood by most Gaelic speakers. Two phonetic version of *Quinag* corresponding to commonly used pronunciations are 'Kwinyak' and 'Coonyak'. The latter is based on an older spelling *Cuinneag*, meaning a milking pail, the name being given, because from certain points (but we have never found them) the mountain is thought to have the shape of an old-fashioned milking pail. Phonetic versions for two other prominent feature are 'Stack Powly' for *Stac Pollaidh* and 'Skoor an Eelir' for Sgurr an Fhidhleir. You may feel happier with the anglicised versions, Stac Polly and The Fiddler.

In general *Fh* at the beginning of a Gaelic word is silent. *Bh* and *Mh* are usually pronounced as V, while *Th* at the beginning of a word is pronounced H, whereas at the middle or end of a word it is often silent. E.g. *Strath* is usually pronounced 'Stra' and *Liath* as 'Lee-a'. Generally, local residents are happy to help visitors with pronunciation.

Words like *mor, beag, Inver, Allt, Bad, Bal, Dun,* etc. often recur. Here is a glossary of such terms, mostly of Gaelic origin:

Aber	Mouth of a river. Used also in Wales. See also *Inver*.
Ach, Auch	Field.
Allt, Alt, Ault	Burn or stream.
Ard, Aird	Promontory or high point
Bad	Grove or thicket.
Bal	Homestead or small settlement.
Bealach	Pass or saddle.
Beg, Beag	Small, little.
Beinn, Ben	Mountain.
Beith	Birch tree.
Binnean	Pinnacle.
Breac	Spotted.
Buidhe	Golden, yellow.
Camas, Camus	Bay or creek (or bend in a river).
Carn	Cairn or heap of stones.
Cioch	Pap.
Clach	Stone.
Creag, Craig	Rock, cliff.
Cul	The back.
Dearg	Red.
Drem, Drom Drum	Ridge (or back in this sense)
Dubh, Dhu	Black or dark.
Dun	Hill or hill-fort.
Eas	Waterfall.
Eilean	Island.
Fad, Fhada	Long.
Fionn	White (or clear).
Garbh	Rough.
Glas	Grey or pale.
Gleann	Glen.
Gorm	Blue or bluish-green.
Inch	Riverside meadow, or small island.
Inver, Inbhir	Mouth of a river. See also *Aber*.
Knock, Cnoc	Knoll or hillock.
Kyle, Caolas	Strait or narrow.
Leathad, Led	Slope.
Liath	Grey.
Loch	Inland lake or sea inlet.
Lochan	Small lake.
Meall	Knob or rounded hill.
Monadh	Moor or heath.
Mor, More, Mohr	Large.
Pol, Poll	Pit or pool.
Rubha, Rudha, Rhu	A promontory.
Sail	Heel.
Sgorr, sgurr	Peak or conical rock.
Stac	Steep rock or conical hill.
Strath	Broad valley.
Stob	Peak or point.
Tarbet, Tarbat	Isthmus.
Torr	Mound or heap.
Uamh	Cave or grave.

A few Viking or Norse words used in names of features in or near *Suilven's World* include:

Ay, Ey	Island.	*Stack*	Columnar rock.
Bard	Extremity, headland.	*Stor, Stour*	Great or large.
		Suil	Pillar.
Lax	Salmon.	*Suther*	Southern.
Ness	Cape or headland.		

Many Norse words used freely in the Northern and Western Isles, e.g. *Papa, Voe, Vik* are less common in mainland Scotland.

Finally in this appendix we give some names of places and features with their approximate English equivalents.

Achmelvich	Field of the sand dunes.
Achiltibuie	Field of the golden boy (but this is not univerally accepted).
Allt nan Uamh	The burn of the caves.
Ardvreck	Speckled point.
Assynt	The ridge end.
Badnaban	Grove of the women.
Ben Mor Coigach	Big mountain of the fifth part.
Ben More Assynt	The big mountain of Assynt.
Caisteal Liath	The grey castle.
Cam Loch	The bent loch.
Clachtoll	The split stone.
Coigach	Place of the fifth part [of a davach?].
Cul Beag	The small back.
Culkein	The back of the headland.
Cul Mor	The big back.
Culnacraig	The back of the cliff.
Drumbeg	The little ridge.
Eas a' Chual Aluinn	The fine waterfall of Glencoul.
Elphin (Elfionn)	The white stone.
Fionn Loch	The white loch.
Glas Bheinn	The grey mountain.
Inchnadamph	Riverside field of the ox.
Inverkirkaig	The church at the mouth of the river.
Knockan	The hillock.

Kylesku	The narrows.
Ledmore	The big slope.
Loch an Leothard	The loch of the steep hill.
Loch Borralan	Loch of the waves.
Loch Dubh	The dark loch.
Lochan Fada	The long lochan.
Lochinver	The (sea) loch at the river mouth.
Loch Lurgainn	The shank loch.
Nedd	The nest.
Polbain	The white pit or pool.
Quinag	The milking pail.
Sail Gharbh	The rough heel.
Sail Gorm	The blue heel.
Sgurr an Fhidhleir	Peak of the fiddler.
Spidean Coinich	The mossy peak.
Stac Pollaidh	The steep hill of the peat bog.
Stoer	The large stack.
Tralligill	The giant's ravine.

The last two are of Viking origin.

Further Reading

We have divided our list into sections, each covering different types of book. Many of the books cover a wide geographical area — some the whole of the Highlands and Islands, and some all of Scotland. We have included a few books that we know to be out of print; we have listed them because we believe they are important or of special interest, and it is often possible still to obtain copies from libraries, secondhand booksellers, or you may even find them on the bookshelves of a friend.

General Guides

A fine general guide to Assynt produced with the support of the Assynt Tourism Group is:

Land of Rocks and Lochs — A Guide to Assynt and Lochinver. Galatea (UK) Ltd., 1993.

Other useful general accounts are included in:

Making More of Assynt. Bill Ritchie, Assynt Mountain Rescue Team.

and in some books on the Highlands including:

The Empty Lands. Tom Atkinson. Luath Press Ltd., 1994.

Three booklets of local area interest, all by Anne Barnes, and published by Eagle Eye Press, have the self-explanatory titles:

Achiltibuie
The Summer Isles
Ullapool.

There are many collections of photographs and sketches of Highland scenes with varying amounts of descriptive text. Perhaps the best-known works in this category are the several books by the late W.A. Poucher and by the late A. Wainright, but preferences between such books is a matter of personal taste, and new volumes appear each year, so we make no firm recommendations.

Walkers' Guides

The Scottish Mountaineering Club publish, and periodically revise, guides for hill-climbing, mountaineering and rock climbing for various regions including the Northern and Western Highlands. These often include details of a range of ascent routes of varying difficulty and are essential books for the specialist climber. However, for the average visitor interested in walking we recommend, according to your interests, one or more of the following. Most of these cover a wider area (usually all Scottish Hills, or hills in specific categories or a selection of hill and coast walks in a particular area).

The Corbetts and Other Scottish Hills. SMC Hillwalkers' Guide, Vol II. Eds. Scott Johnstone, Hamish Brown and Donald Bennet. Scottish Mountaineering Trust, 1990.

The Corbett Almanac. Cameron McNeish. Neil Wilson Publishing, 1994.

The Munros. SMC Hillwalkers' Guide. Vol I. Ed. Donald Bennet. Scottish Mountaineering Trust, 1985.

The Munro Almanac. Cameron McNeish. Neil Wilson Publishing, 1991.

Climbing the Corbetts. Hamish M. Brown. Victor Gollancz Ltd., 1988.

West Highland Walks: Two, Skye to Cape Wrath. Hamish MacInnes. Hodder and Stoughton.

The Scottish Peaks. W.A. Poucher. Constable & Co. 1974.

100 Best Routes on Scottish Mountains. Ralph Storer. David & Charles, 1987.

For information about estates and access and general guidance on using the countryside you should have the most recent edition of the frequently revised

Heading for the Scottish Hills compiled by the Mountaineering Council for Scotland and the Scottish Landowners' Federation. Scottish Mountaineering Trust.

An amusing account of mountain climbing is

The First Fifty —Munro Bagging Without a Beard. Muriel Gray. Mainstream, 1991.

History and archaeology

The books listed below cover more than just Suilven's World. There is also coverage of various aspects of local history in some of the guides listed on p. 145. In particular in *Land of Rocks and Lochs* and in the 3 booklets by Anne Barnes.

Guide to Prehistoric Scotland. Richard Feachem. R.T. Batsford, 1977.

Prehistoric Lochbroom & Assynt. Cathy Dagg. Lochbroom Field Club, 1990.

Crofts and Crofting. Katharine Stewart. James Thin, 1980.

Crofting Years. Francis Thompson. Luath Press, 1993.

Geology

The first four publications listed are ideal introductory works but the last is more detailed and technical. The first item is essentially a folding descriptive leaflet, and it is ideally suited to touring if a quick introduction is wanted.

Assynt Geological Motor Trail. D.R. Shelley. Sutherland Tourist Board.

Geological Trail —Knockan Cliff. Scottish Natural Heritage, 1993.

Highland Landforms. Robert J. Price. Highlands and Islands Development Board, 1976. (Reprinted 1991 by Aberdeen University Press).

Geology and Scenery in Scotland. J. B. Whittow. Penguin Books Ltd, 1977.

British Regional Geology — The Northern Highlands of Scotland. 4th Ed. G.S. Johnstone and W. Mykura. British Geological Survey. HMSO, 1989.

Flora and Fauna

There are a lot of books dealing particularly with birds or with specific types of flora such as trees, shrubs, fungi, etc. often covering areas such as Scotland, the British Isles or even Northern Europe. We list only a few, but many more are available in bookshops. The first two books below are local, the others of wider interest, but all are relevant to *Suilven's World*.

An Introduction to the Flowering Plants and Ferns of Loch Broom & Assynt. Colin Scouller. Lochbroom Field Club, 1988.

Knockan Cliff Nature Trail. Scottish Natural Heritage, 1992.

Highland Birds. D. Nethersole-Thompson. Highlands and Islands Development Board, 1971.

Highland Flora. Derek Ratcliffe. Highlands and Islands Development Board, 1977.

Highland Animals. David Stephen. Highlands and Islands Development Board, 1974.

Wildlife of Scotland. Ed. Fred Holliday. MacMillan, London, 1979.

The Highlands & Islands. F. Fraser Darling & J. Morton Boyd. Collins, 1969.

The Concise British Flora in Colour. W. Keble Martin. Ebury Press/Michael Joseph, 1965.

The Illustrated Flora of Britain and Northern Europe. Marjorie Blamey and Christopher Grey-Wilson. Hodder & Stoughton, 1989.

The Wildflower Key, British Isles — N.W. Europe. Francis Rose. Frederick Warne, 1981.
The Oxford Book of Insects. John Burton. Oxford University Press, 1968.
A Field Guide to the Insects of Britain and Northern Europe. Michael Chinery. Collins, 1985.
The Oxford Book of Flowerless Plants. F.H. Brightman and B.E. Nicholson. Oxford University Press, 1966.
John Anthony's Flora of Sutherland. Ed. J. B. Kenworthy. Botanical Society of Edinburgh, 1976.
The Grasses, Ferns, Mosses & Lichens of Great Britain and Ireland. Roger Phillips. Pan Books, 1980.
The World of Mushrooms. Uberto Tosco. Orbis, 1973.

Visitors with no previous angling experience may find the following introductory guide useful if tempted to try their hands:

The Essential Guide to Trout Fishing. Michael Brander. Canongate, 1992.

Maps

We list some relevant sheets of the Ordnance Survey Landranger series. The scale is 2 cm = 1 km (approximately 1.25 in. = 1 mile). The Ordnance Survey and Bartholomew also produce maps on other scales (giving more or less detail) and special geological maps are also published. There are, in addition, the many, and mostly good, road atlases available for motorists.

Landranger sheet 9. Cape Wrath.
Landranger sheet 15. Loch Assynt & surrounding area.
Landranger sheet 16. Lairg, Loch Shin & surrounding area.
Landranger sheet 19. Gairloch & Ullapool areas.
Landranger sheet 20. Beinn Dearg.

Miscellaneous books

The books listed below in some cases only refer briefly to matters relevant to *Suilven's World*, but all are interesting books about specific Scottish features.

A Guide to the Nature Reserves of Scotland. Linda Bennett. MacMillan, London, 1989.

A History of Scotland. J.D. Mackie. Penguin Books, 1977.

Scottish Place Names. A.M. Eyers. Sphere Books Ltd, 1983.

The Waterfalls of Scotland. Louis Stott. Aberdeen University press, 1987.

Highland Bridges. Gillian Nelson. Aberdeen University Press, 1990

Index